The *Illustrated* VOYAGE OF THE BEAGLE

A Novel Adaptation of Charles Darwin's Classic

Book 1

The Voyage Begins

Collect the Complete Series

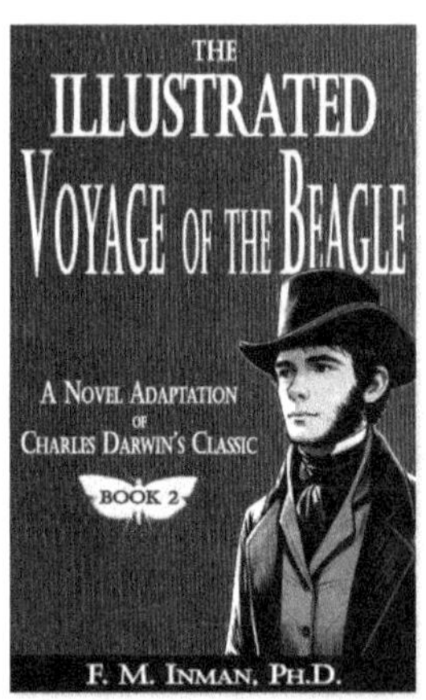

The Illustrated VOYAGE OF THE BEAGLE

A Novel Adaptation of Charles Darwin's Classic

Book 1
The Voyage Begins

F.M. Inman, Ph.D.

Published by Rainforest Kids

NORTH AMERICA
ATLANTIC
PACIFIC
OCEAN
OCEAN
Sandwich Isles
Marquesas
Navigators
Friendly I.
Society Islands
Low or Dangerous Archipelago
SOUTH AMERICA
Galapagos Islands
R. of Panama
R. Amazon
S. Paul Rocks
Fernando Noronha
Pernambuco
Callao & Lima
Bahia
Arica
Iquique
St. Helena
Rio Janeiro
I. S. Catharina
Copiapo
Coquimbo
Valparaiso
Santiago
Juan Fernandez
Buenos Ayres
Monte Video
Maldonado
R. de la Plata
Conception
Valdivia
Blanco B.
Rio Negro
Chiloe
Chonos Archip.
Port Desire
R. S. Cruz
Falkland Islands
Str. of Magellan
Sea of Magalhaens
Staten I.
Chanar I.
C. Horn
Sandwich Islands
New South Shetland

ATLANTIC
OCEAN
Labrador
Newfoundland
Nova Scotia
ENGLAND
London
Lands End
Bay of Biscay
FRANCE
C. Finisterre
Western Isles
Str. of Gibraltar
SPAIN
Western Isles
SPAIN
Madeira
Canary Is.
Teneriffe
C. Verd Is.
C. Verd
C. Palmas

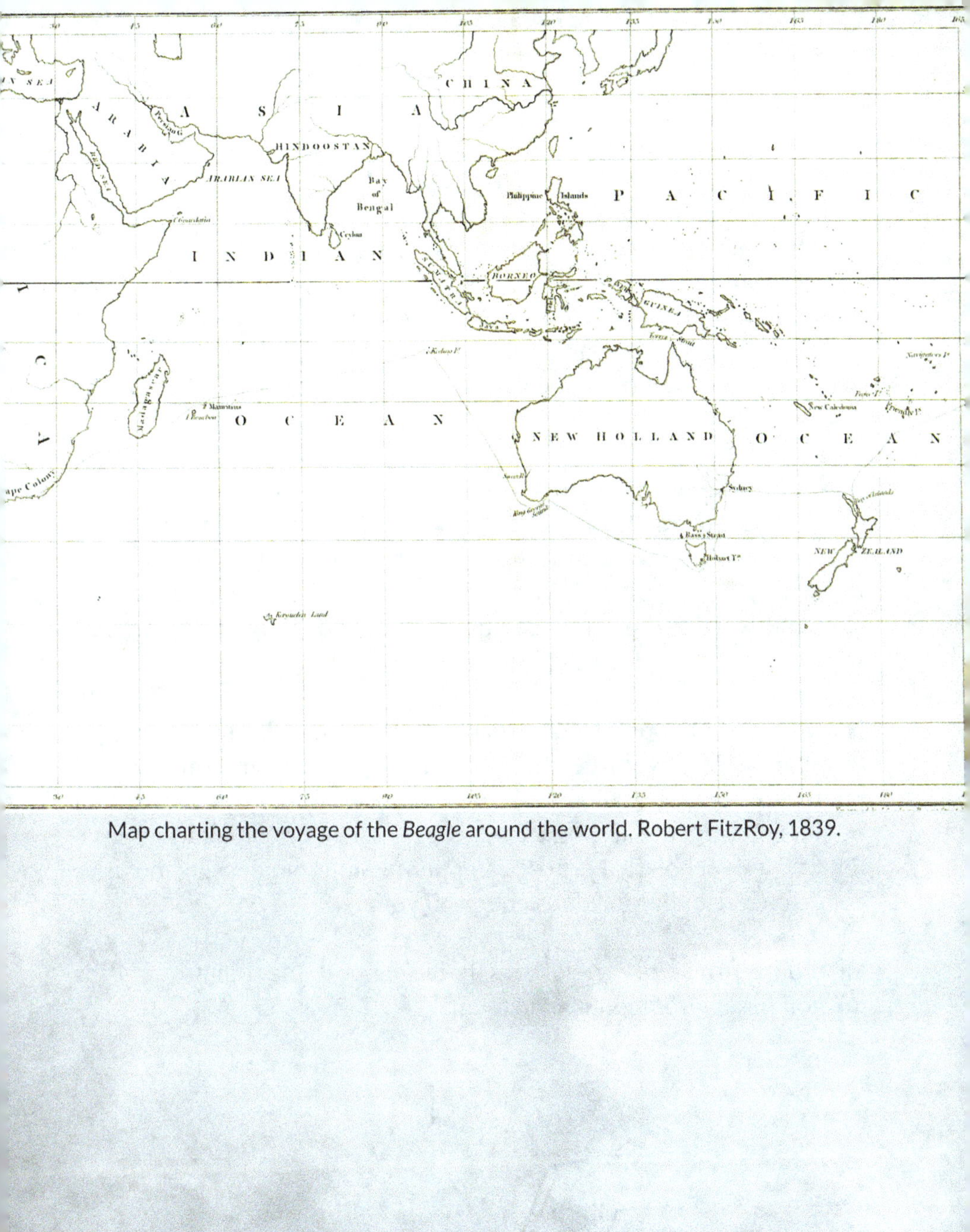

Map charting the voyage of the *Beagle* around the world. Robert FitzRoy, 1839.

Published by Rainforest Kids

ISBN
979-8-9916442-3-5

Table of Contents

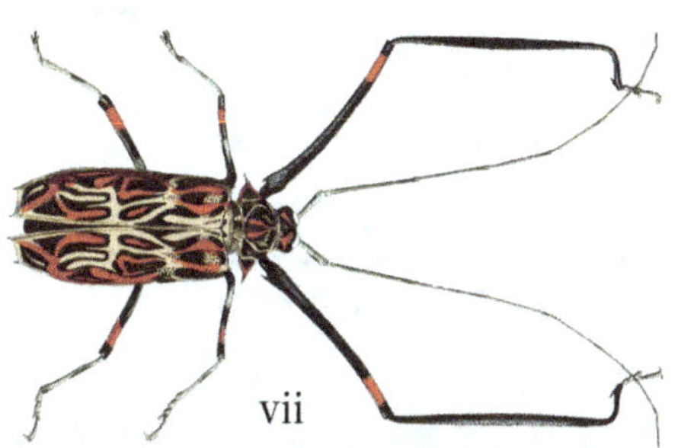

*For my mother, who asked me why I was doing this,
which is a very good question.*

Introduction

This book presents a revised version of the first three chapters of *The Voyage of the Beagle*, the travel journal Charles Darwin wrote while sailing around the world as the ship's naturalist aboard the H.M.S. *Beagle*. Darwin's journey changed his thinking, and his thinking changed the world. His travels led directly to the development of his theory of evolution by natural selection—the foundation of modern biology.

Darwin wrote an entertaining account, but his old-fashioned language can be difficult to understand. To make his story accessible and enjoyable for everyone, I rewrote the text while staying true to its original content and spirit. In this adaptation, I updated the names of places he visited and species he encountered. I also added over a hundred historically and scientifically accurate images so you can picture the plants, animals, landscapes, and people he saw.

This first book in the series is relatively short but especially rich in adventure. In Chapter One, 22-year-old Charles leaves wintry England and explores tropical islands as he crosses the Atlantic Ocean. He strolls happily under palm trees on the Cabo Verde Islands, puzzles over the unique geology of St. Paul's Rocks, and catalogs the animals of remote Fernando de Noronha. In Chapter Two, he ventures into Brazil, where he is awed by the beauty and biodiversity of the rainforest. In Chapter Three, he rides across the pampas, chasing rheas with *gauchos* in Uruguay. Future books in this series will continue to follow his journey as he circles the globe, exploring nature and culture along the way.

I hope you'll be as delighted as I am by Darwin's adventurous spirit, curiosity, humor, and insights. Reading his story inspires me to see the world in a new way—I hope it will inspire you, too!

F. M. Inman, Ph.D.
Río Claro, Costa Rica
March 14, 2025

Black noddy (*Anous hawaiiensis*). Frederick William Frohawk, c. 1890.

Preface

I wish to express my deep gratitude to Captain FitzRoy, who invited me on this journey to serve as the ship's naturalist. All the opportunities I enjoyed to study the natural history of the various countries we visited were due entirely to him. Not only did he generously give up part of his own accommodations to make room for me, but he also offered me warm friendship and unwavering support throughout our five years together. I will always be deeply thankful to Captain FitzRoy and all the officers of the *Beagle* for their consistent kindness during our long voyage. I must also express my sincere gratitude to the *Beagle*'s doctor, Benjamin Bynoe, who kindly cared for me when I was very ill in Valparaíso.

Likewise, I am pleased to acknowledge the invaluable support I received from many other naturalists and offer my heartfelt thanks to the Reverend Professor Henslow, who first inspired my interest in natural history when I was an undergraduate at Cambridge. He not only cared for the collections I sent home, but also sent me letters that guided my work throughout the voyage. Since my return, he has continued to offer me the generous support of a true friend.

Finally, I thank Captain Francis Beaufort, the hydrographer, for helping me secure approval for the journey from the Lords of the Admiralty.

This volume presents the history of our voyage in the form of a journal, outlining my observations on natural history and geology, which I believe will interest readers. For this edition, I have condensed and revised certain sections and added a few details to make it more accessible to a general audience.

I encourage readers with a deeper interest in natural history to consult the other publications from our expedition, which contain the full scientific results. For these works, I am indebted to the exceptional talents and dedication of the contributing authors. Their publications were made possible by a generous grant of £1,000 ($100,000 in today's dollars) from the Lords Commissioners of Her Majesty's Treasury, provided through the Right Honourable Chancellor of the Exchequer to cover publication costs.

Charles Darwin
Down, Bromley, Kent
June 9, 1845

CHAPTER 1
ACROSS THE ATLANTIC

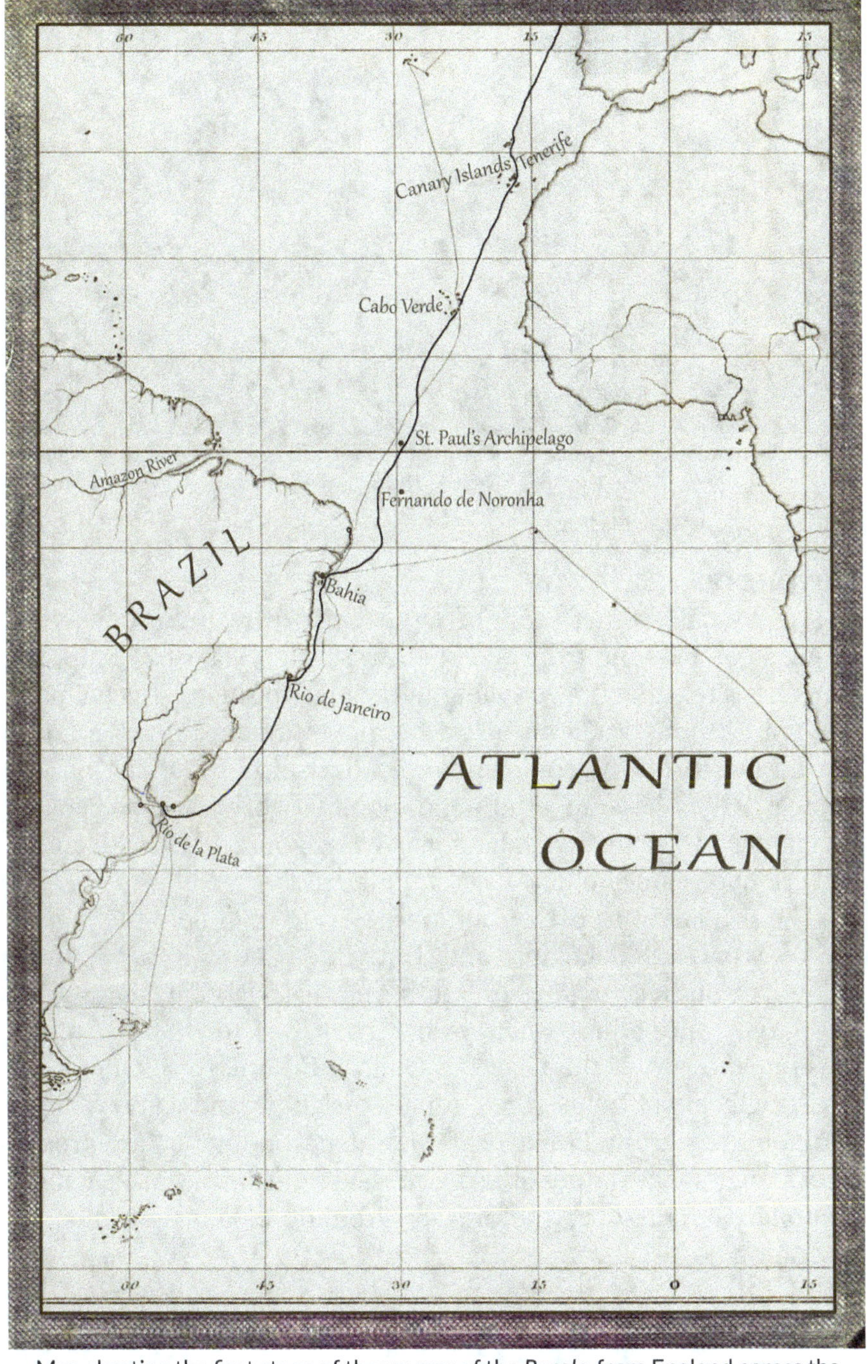

Map charting the first stage of the voyage of the *Beagle*, from England across the Atlantic to Brazil. Robert FitzRoy, 1839.

Departing England

Sailing from England after twice being driven back by heavy winter storms. William Watts, 1803.

December 27, 1831

Devonport

At last, we sail from Devonport after being driven back twice by heavy gales blowing from the southwest. Her Majesty's Ship, the *Beagle*, is a ten-gun brig, a sailing ship with two square-rigged masts and ten cannons. I am on board because Captain Robert FitzRoy invited me to be his companion and the ship's naturalist on this voyage. My job is to study the natural world and to collect specimens of the plants and animals we encounter. Our adventure will last five years and take us around the globe.

The primary purpose of our journey is to complete the map of the coastlines of Patagonia and Tierra del Fuego, two relatively unknown southern regions of South America. Captain King started this survey during an earlier voyage from 1826 to 1830. Next, our mission is to survey the coasts of Chile and Peru, travel across the Pacific Ocean to map some remote islands, and carry marine chronometers around the world. Marine chronometers are precise clocks that make it possible to measure distances at sea more accurately than ever before—a groundbreaking advance in navigation.

Canary Islands

The sunrise suddenly illuminates the peak of Mt. Teide on the first of many delightful days never to be forgotten. Jules Marie Vincent de Sinéty, 1837.

January 6, 1832

Tenerife

After ten days of sailing hundreds of miles to the southwest, we reach the island of Tenerife. This is the largest of the Canary Islands, located off the western shores of northern Africa. Sadly, we are not allowed to land because they fear we might bring cholera, a deadly disease that arrived in Britain by ship last year and killed many thousands of people.

In the early morning, we watch the sunrise from the deck of the ship. As the sun peaks out from behind the rugged outline of Gran Canaria Island, it suddenly illuminates the volcanic peak of Mt. Teide in glowing red light, while the lower hillsides remain hidden under fleecy clouds. This is the first of many delightful days that I will never forget.

Cabo Verde Islands

Cone-shaped hills and rugged mountains of Porto Praia, Island of Santiago. William Alexander, 1806.

January 16, 1832

Porto Praia

Another ten days of sailing to the south by southwest brings us to Porto Praia, a small town on the island of Santiago, the largest in the Cabo Verde archipelago, off the northwest coast of Africa.

As we approach Porto Praia from the sea, the land looks desolate. The soil, shaped by volcanic fires of ages past, is so scorched under the heat of the tropical sun that it supports little vegetation.

The landscape is made up of table-lands that rise in giant steps, interspersed with short, cone-shaped hills. A rugged chain of high mountains defines the horizon line. The climate makes the atmosphere hazy, rendering the scene all the more picturesque. Though, as I am fresh from the sea, walking for the first time in a grove of coconut trees, I can hardly be a judge of anything but my own happiness.

Some people might find the island uninteresting. But, as I am only accustomed to English landscapes, the novelty of this utterly sterile land has a grandeur that might be spoiled by more vegetation. I can scarcely discover a single green leaf across the wide lava plains. Yet herds of goats and a few cows manage to subsist here. It seldom rains, but heavy torrents fall during the short rainy season. After the rains, bright plants spring out of every crack in the ground. The plants quickly dry and wither, forming a natural hay that the animals live on for the rest of the year. It has been an entire year since the last rain.

The area around Porto Praia was covered in trees when Europeans first visited it. But people recklessly cut them down and now the land is almost entirely barren. Forests on other islands, such as St. Helena and most of the Canary Islands, were also destroyed in this way. I learned this only much later from Dr. Ernst Dieffenbach, who translated my book into German.

On Santiago, the wide, flat valleys channel the seasonal rains that come for only a few days a year. Now, these dry valleys are clothed with thickets of leafless bushes, and few animals live here.

The most common bird I see is a colorful kingfisher (*Halcyon leucocephala*). It perches tamely on the branches of a castor-oil plant, waiting to catch grasshoppers and lizards. Its feathers are bright, but not as beautiful as those of the European kingfisher. Its behavior and habitat are also different; it lives in the driest valleys, far from the rivers and streams where its European cousins are found.

The most common bird is a grey-headed kingfisher (*Halcyon leucocephala*) that perches tamely on the branches of a castor-oil plant waiting to catch grasshoppers and lizards. John Gerrard Keulemans, 1868.

The ancient capital of Santiago, showing the cathedral, bishop's palace and view from the garden of a ruined convent. George Henry Mowbray, 1839.

Ribeira Grande

One day, I ride with two officers to Ribeira Grande, a village a few miles east of Porto Praia. As we travel, the countryside looks dry and brown until we reach the valley of St. Martin. Here, a very small rill of water produces refreshingly luxuriant vegetation along its banks.

After about an hour of riding, we arrive in Ribeira Grande where we are surprised by the sight of a ruined fort and cathedral. This town was the most important place on the island until its harbor filled up with sediment. The town is still picturesque, but these days it appears sad and melancholy.

We hire two guides: a black priest (here called a *padre*) and a Spanish interpreter who had served in the Peninsular War when the British sided with Spain against Napoleon. Together, we explore an ancient church and other buildings.

The former governors and captain-generals of the island are buried at the church, and some tombstones date back to the 16th century. One grave is marked with the date 1571. Another tombstone bears a crest of a hand and a dagger from 1497. The Cabo Verde Islands were first found by Europeans in 1449, so this tombstone may mark one of the oldest graves on the island. These carved stones are the only things here that remind us of Europe.

The church forms one side of a square courtyard. On another side of the courtyard is a hospital in which there are twelve or so miserable-looking patients. A large clump of bananas grows in the center of the courtyard.

For dinner, we return to the local *venda* (the Portuguese word for inn). A crowd of dark-skinned men, women, and children gather to watch us eat. They are extremely merry and laugh heartily at everything we do.

We visit the cathedral before leaving the town. It is larger than the church, but appears less rich. It is proud of its little organ, which cries out in a uniquely inharmonious manner when played.

We give the priest a few coins in payment. Then the Spanish interpreter pats him on the head and candidly tells him that his skin color makes no difference. At last, we ride back to Porto Praia as swiftly as our ponies can carry us.

A Ride to São Domingos

Another day, we ride to the village of São Domingos, located near the center of the island. On the way, we cross a small plain where a few stunted *Acacia* trees grow. The steady trade winds bend the *Acacia* branches sideways, some even at right angles to their trunks. These prevailing winds are so consistent that the direction of the branches serves as natural wind vanes, clearly showing which way the wind blows—northeast by north and southwest by south.

After the gloomy scenery of the rest of the island, the unexpected beauty of São Domingos surprises us. The village is located at the bottom of a valley surrounded by tall, jagged walls

Guinea fowl (*Agelastes meleagrides*). Daniel Giraud Elliot, 1870.

formed by layers upon layers of lava rock. The black rocks contrast strikingly with the bright green vegetation that lines the riverbanks.

The day we visit happens to be a feast day and the village is full of people celebrating. On our way back, we pass a group of about twenty young black girls. They are tastefully dressed in white linen with colorful turbans and large shawls. When we approach, they suddenly turn toward us and block the rocky path with their shawls. They energetically sing a wild song, clapping and beating time on their legs. We toss them some *vintems*—small coins—which they accept with laughter and sing twice as loud as we ride away.

Our passage leaves no tracks in the barren soil, so we accidentally take the wrong path back. We only realize our error when we arrive in the nearby village of Fuentes. However, this turns out to be a pleasant mistake. Fuentes is a pretty little village with a small stream and lush plants. The town looks prosperous, except for what most should be prosperous: the people. The black children are completely naked and wretched, carrying bundles of firewood half the size of their own bodies.

Near Fuentes, we see a large flock of about 50–60 guinea fowl. We are unable to get close to these extremely wary birds. They run from us with heads cocked up, like partridges on a rainy September day, and quickly fly away if we chase them.

A Remarkably Clear Morning with Dry Air

One morning, the view from the *Beagle* is exceptionally clear. The distant mountains are outlined sharply against a heavy bank of dark blue clouds. Lightning flashes constantly. From this, I think the air must be extremely humid, as is often the case in England.

However, the facts show that I am wrong. When I use a hygrometer to measure the amount of moisture in the air, I find that the air temperature would have to be nearly 30°F lower for moisture to condense from the air. This means that the air is unusually dry, more so than on any of the previous mornings. Is it common to see such remarkably dry and transparent air alongside such stormy weather?

Atmospheric Dust Full of Microscopic Life

The air around the Cabo Verde Islands is generally hazy. I discover that this haze comes from incredibly fine dust falling from the sky. The morning before we anchor at Porto Praia, I collect a little packet of this brown dust that was filtered from the wind by the gauze of the ship's vane at the top of the *Beagle's* mast. Charles Lyell, the eminent geologist, also gives me four packets of dust that fell on a ship a few hundred miles north of Cabo Verde. Professor Christian Gottfried Ehrenberg, an expert on microscopic life, kindly examines these packets of dust. He finds that the dust is mostly made of diatoms and other microorganisms with hard silica shells and bits of silica from plants. In just five small packets, Professor Ehrenberg finds 67 different types of life! Surprisingly, all but two of the microorganisms come from freshwater, not the ocean.

Based on the wind direction and the time of year when the dust falls, we can be sure that it all comes from Africa, carried by the Harmattan—strong winds which raise clouds of dust high into the atmosphere. This is why it is puzzling that Professor Ehrenberg, who knows the African diatoms very well, finds none of the familiar African species in the dust I send him. Rather, he finds two species which he previously only knows to live in South America. How these species end up in African dust is a mystery.

The dust falls in such large amounts that it dirties everything on board and hurts the sailor's eyes. It is so fine that it enters and slightly damages our astronomical instruments. Ships even run aground when the air becomes dark with this dust.

This dust is so light that it floats on the wind and often travels great distances. I later find 15 different reports of dust containing these microorganisms falling on ships far out in the Atlantic Ocean. These reports state that it frequently falls on ships several hundred, or even more than a thousand miles, from shore. It is reportedly found on ships as far as 1,600 miles from the African coast. In one dust sample I collect 300 miles from land, I am surprised to find particles of stone as large as 1000th of an inch square mixed in with the finer dust. Knowing this fact, it no longer surprises me that the much lighter and smaller spores of cryptogamic plants, such as ferns and mosses, can spread so widely.

Freshwater ciliates in the genus *Dictyocysta* identified by Professor Ehrenberg. William Saville-Kent, 1880.

Santiago Island Geology

The geology is the most interesting part of Santiago Island's natural history. As we enter the harbor, I see a perfectly horizontal band of white stone running across the face of the sea cliff. This band is elevated about 45 feet above the water and stretches for miles along the coast.

When I examine it closely, I find that this white layer, or stratum, is made of a chalky, calcareous stone. There are many shells embedded in it. Most of these shells still exist on the nearby shore today, suggesting that the origin of this white stone is relatively recent. This white layer lies on top of ancient volcanic basalt rocks and is covered by a second layer of younger basalt rocks. I imagine that a stream of lava must have flowed into the sea and over a bed of white seashells while it was lying at the bottom of the ocean.

It is interesting to follow the ancient tracks where the heat of the lava flowing over the chalky white stone transformed it. The crumbly mass became crystalline limestone in some places and a compact spotted stone in others. In places where the chalky stone is covered by rough, porous fragments of lava it was converted into beautifully radiating crystals.

If you look inland, you can see how the lava flows form gently sloping plains, rising higher and higher toward the center of the island where the lava originated. Though the island is volcanic, there have been no eruptions in recorded history. Few of the hills made of red cinders—small, rough lava rocks—have craters. However, you can still see differences between older and newer lava flows along the coast. The newer ones form low cliffs that stick out far into the sea. By comparing the height of these cliffs, you can roughly estimate which flows are older and which are more recent.

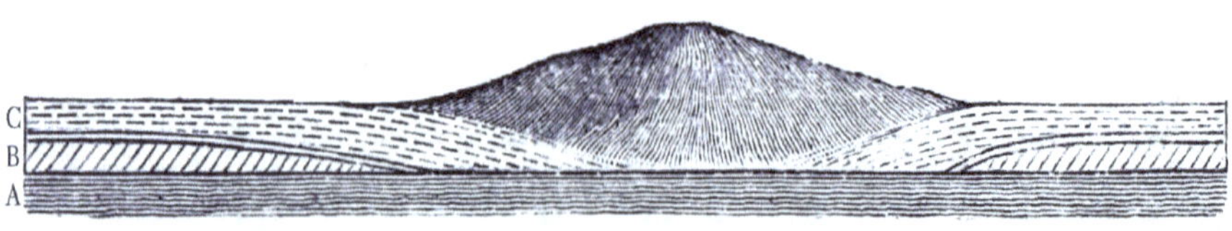

Signal Post hill reveals striking rock layers: A) ancient volcanic rocks, B) chalky white layer with embedded seashells, and C) younger volcanic rocks. Charles Darwin, 1844.

Sea-slug in the genus *Aplysia*. Alcide d'Orbigny, 1835.

Behavior of a Sea Slug & Octopus

I enjoy observing the behavior of marine animals in Santiago. One of the most common creatures I find here is a sea slug in the genus *Aplysia*. This animal is about five inches long, with a dirty yellowish body veined in purple. It has broad membranes running along each side of the lower part of its body which appear to help it breathe by causing a current of water to flow over its lungs.

The sea slug feeds on delicate seaweeds that grow among stones in shallow, muddy water. When I examine its stomach contents, I find tiny pebbles, similar to what you might find in a bird's gizzard. When disturbed, the sea slug produces a fine, purple-red liquid that spreads through the surrounding water, making a cloud to hide itself. It also defends itself by secreting a chemical all over its body that stings as much as the Portuguese man-of-war (a large jellyfish in the genus *Physalia*).

I am particularly fascinated by the behavior of an octopus, also called a cuttlefish. Though common in the small pools left behind by the tide, it is very hard to catch. The octopus uses its long arms and powerful suckers to wedge itself into narrow cracks in the rocks. Once in place, it takes great force to pull it out. I watch as it shoots through the water tail-first, as quickly as an arrow, while releasing a dark chestnut-brown ink, which makes the water murky.

This animal is remarkable at hiding itself. It has an extraordinary ability to change color, much like a chameleon. It can even rapidly alter its color to match the ground as it passes over. The octopus shows its chameleon-like ability to change color both while swimming and while sitting still on the bottom of the pool.

I am much amused by the many tricks played by one individual. In deep water, I see its skin turn a dark brownish purple. In shallow water or on land, it becomes a pale yellowish green. Looking more closely, I realize that its base color is really a French grey with many tiny bright yellow spots. The shades of grey constantly change while the yellow spots appear and disappear. The colors continuously shift like clouds moving across its body, creating colors that range from hyacinth red to chestnut brown. They say that the clouds of colors are made by expansion and contraction of small sacs in the skin called chromatophores that contain different colored fluids (Owen 1836).

This octopus seems to know that I am watching. To evade me, it stays still for a time, then stealthily inches forward like a cat after a mouse, sometimes changing its color as it advances. When it reaches a deeper part of the pool, it darts away, leaving a dusky trail of ink to hide the hole it crawls into.

As I lean low over the rocky shore looking for marine life, I am more than once surprised to be saluted by a sudden jet of water. I am confused by this at first, but I soon realize it is this same octopus. Though concealed in a hole, the jets of water lead me to its hiding place. Not only does it have the power to squirt water using the siphon on the underside of its body, it also appears to have the ability to take good aim.

When I pick it up and place it on land, the octopus struggles to move because its head is difficult to carry. I also see that it turns black when I apply a small electric shock to it or scratch it with a needle. I keep one alive in the ship's cabin where it gives off a faint, phosphorescent light in the dark.

Saint Peter and Saint Paul Archipelago

St. Paul's remote cluster of rocky islets is geologically complex and unique. Charles Wyville Thomson, 1877.

February 16, 1832

While crossing the Atlantic, we pause near the remote Saint Peter and Saint Paul Archipelago (St. Paul's, for short). This tiny cluster of rocky islets rises abruptly from the depths of the ocean. The highest point is only 50 feet above sea level and the total circumference, when traced all around the edges of the shores, is less than three-quarters of a mile. It is located nearly halfway between Africa and South America, just above the equator (1° north latitude and 29° west longitude). It is 350 miles away from the island of Fernando de Noronha and 540 miles from the coast of South America.

St. Paul's geology is remarkably complex. In some parts, the rocks are made of chert, which is a hard sedimentary rock made from smaller particles of stone that have solidified over time. In other parts, the rocks are feldspar with thin veins of green serpentine. This type of rock comes from magma which solidifies far below the surface of the earth. This combination of rock types makes St. Paul's unique. Almost all small islands located far from continents—whether in the Pacific, Indian, or Atlantic Oceans—are made of either coral (created by tiny sea creatures) or volcanic rock (formed by lava). The only exceptions I know are the Seychelles and St. Paul.

I do not fully understand St. Paul's geology. However, I know that the explanation for its unique volcanic nature must follow the same laws that we use to explain why most active volcanoes are located near coastlines or as islands in the midst of the sea.

Singular Incrustations

St. Paul's rocks shine brightly white when I see them from a distance. This unusual color comes partly from the dung of a vast number of seabirds and partly from a hard, glossy coating with a pearly shine that sticks to the rock surfaces. When I examine this white coating closely with a magnifying lens, I see that it is made up of many extremely thin layers, altogether about 1/10th of an inch thick. It contains mostly animal matter and doubtless forms from the action of the rain or ocean spray on the birds' dung.

Later in the voyage, I see something similar on Ascension Island and on the Abrolhos Islets, where I find small branching structures below clumps of guano. These branches look so much like certain rhodoliths (a type of coral-like sea plant) that I fail to notice the difference when I hastily examine my collection later. The rounded tips of these branches have a pearly texture, like tooth enamel, but are hard enough to scratch glass.

On the coast of Ascension, I also observe a different type of hard mineral covering, or incrustation, on tidal rocks near a large pile of sand made from seashells. This incrustation is created by the movement of seawater against the calcium-rich sand. Thus, it is inorganic, not formed by living creatures. Yet its shape reminds me of liverworts (a small plant that grows in damp places). Also, like a plant, the color of the incrustation depends on how much light it receives: parts exposed to full sunlight are jet black, while those shaded under rock ledges are pale grey.

I am not the only one to be bewildered by this substance. Several geologists I later show it to assume it must come from volcanic activity!

Its resemblance to living seashells is striking. It is as hard, translucent, and polished as the finest oliva shell. This substance also smells bad and loses its color when heated with a blowpipe, similar to living shells. Also like a shell, parts exposed to light are darker, while shaded areas are paler. These similarities are fascinating when we remember that phosphorus and calcium are key minerals in the bird dung, the sand made from seashells, and the hard parts of all living animals, such as bones and shells. How is it that nature can form materials harder than tooth enamel, as polished as fresh shells, and shaped like simple plants, using only non-living minerals?

Observations made by the scientists Leonard Horner and Sir David Brewster show us another example of how inorganic nature mimics life (Horner and Brewster 1836). They found an artificial substance resembling seashell on the inside of a vessel of rapidly spinning cloth that was covered with glue and calcium-rich minerals in water. This process created thin, transparent, polished brown layers with unique optical properties. Although softer and more transparent than the incrustations at Ascension, it shows how calcium-rich minerals tend to make solid substances similar to seashells when combined with animal matter. How curious it is that materials formed by nonliving processes mimic those produced by life!

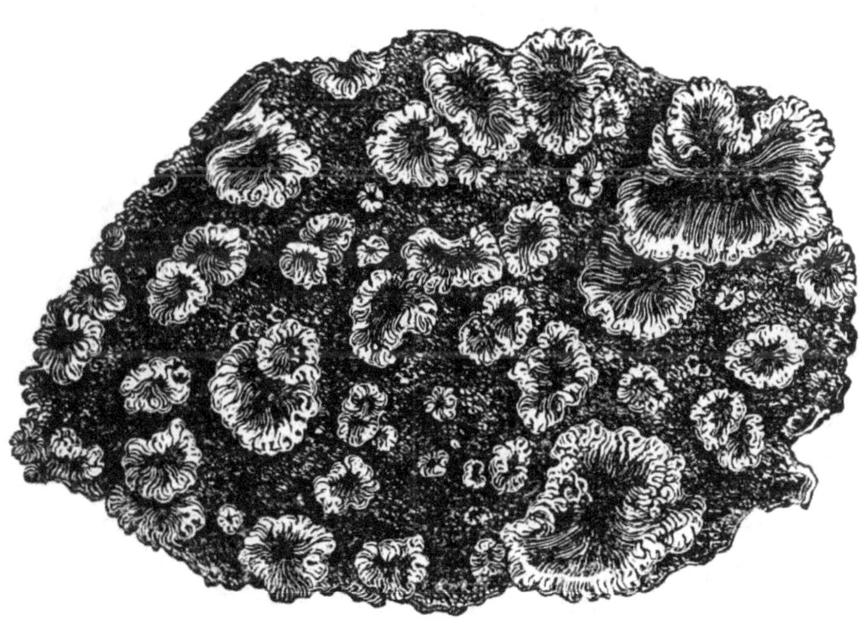

A strange incrustation on the rocks at Ascension shows us that calcium-rich matter combined with mechanical processes can create materials that mirror those made by living creatures. Charles Darwin, 1844.

The black noddy (*Anous minutus*) nests in large flocks on St. Paul's Archipelago. F. O. Morris, 1862.

St. Paul's Birds

On St. Paul's we find only two kinds of birds: the brown booby (*Sula leucogaster*) and the black noddy (*Anous minutus*). The booby is a type of gannet and the noddy is a kind of tern. Both birds are surprisingly tame and stupid. They are so unwary that I can kill as many as I want by knocking them on the head with my geological hammer.

The booby lays its eggs directly on the bare rock without making a nest, while the noddy builds a simple nest out of seaweed. I notice small flying fish next to many of these nests. I suppose the male birds bring these fish as food for their partners.

It is funny to watch how quickly a large and active crab steals a fish from the side of the nest when we disturb the parent birds. These crabs, in the genus *Grapsus*, live in cracks in the rocks and are extremely bold. Sir W. Symonds, one of the few people to land on St. Paul, tells me that he even sees the crabs drag young birds out of their nests to eat them.

The masked booby (*Sula dactylatra*) is one of the booby species that visits St. Paul's Archipelago. John Jennens, 1859.

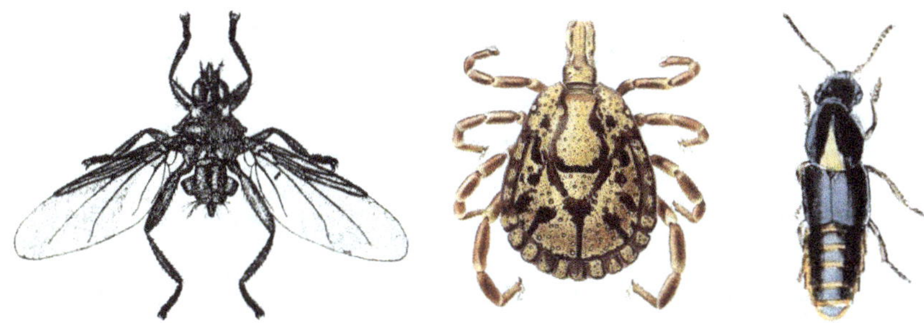

The first colonists on new islands appear to be parasitic flies (*Olfersia* species; Nowonstein, 1905), ticks (*Amblyomma* species; Wilhelm Dönitz, 1908), and beetles that live under dung (*Quedius* species; John Curtis, 1863).

Insects: The First Colonists of Islands

Not a single plant grows on St. Paul, not even lichen. Despite this, the islands are home to several insects and spiders. The often-repeated description of coral islands in the Pacific being first colonized by the stately palm and other noble tropical plants, then by birds, and lastly by man, is wrong. I fear the truth destroys the poetry of the story. But, in fact, insects that feed on feathers and dung, parasites, and spiders are really the first inhabitants of newly formed oceanic islands.

Besides several spider species which prey on the insects, the following is a complete list of all the animals—the entire terrestrial fauna—of the islands:

1. A fly (*Olfersia* species) that lives on the booby birds.
2. A tick (*Amblyomma darwini*), likely brought to the island as a parasite on the birds.
3. A small, brown moth (*Erechthias darwini*) that feeds on feathers.
4. A beetle (*Quedius* species), found beneath bird dung.
5. A woodlouse, also found beneath bird dung.

Fernando de Noronha

Catamaran at Fernando de Noronha. Charles Wyville Thomson, 1878.

February 20, 1832

All I am able to see during the few hours we stay at Fernando de Noronha is that the island is volcanic, but not recently active. The most remarkable feature of the island is a conical hill that rises about 1,000 feet above sea level. Its upper slopes are so steep that one side overhangs its base. The hill is made of phonolite, a volcanic rock that splits into irregular columns, giving it a jagged and dramatic appearance. At first, I thought that the rock overhang was suddenly pushed up as liquid lava. However, at St. Helena, I later see steeply pointed rock pinnacles similar to this one and learned that these were formed by the injection of melted rock into softer layers of rock, which served as molds. These gigantic stone spires remind me of obelisks from ancient Egypt.

Though the island is covered with trees, the climate is so dry that it does not look luxuriant. When I climb halfway up the mountain, I am pleased by the scene of great masses of rock formed into vertical columns. Near the dark rocks are trees that remind me of laurels. They are bare of leaves but are covered with delicate pink flowers.

Fish biodiversity of Saint Peter and Saint Paul's Archipelago. F. M. Inman, 2025.

Fish on Remote Islands

Even the smallest rock in the tropical seas can become the foundation for the growth of many types of seaweed, animals, and fish. I watch as sharks and seamen in boats struggle over who should have the greater share of fish caught by the lines. I have heard of a rock near the Bermudas, far out at sea and at a great depth, that was first discovered because of the large number of fish spotted swimming in the area.

Laelia grandis tenebrosa. Anonymous, 1899.

CHAPTER 2
BRAZIL

Map charting the second stage of the voyage of the *Beagle*, from Brazil south to the Río de la Plata and Uruguay. Robert FitzRoy, 1839.

Bahia

Brazil's delightful tropical forest is a naturalist's dream come true. Bernhard Wiegandt, 1878.

February 29, 1832
Tropical Rainforest

Today is a delightful day, though the word 'delight' feels far too weak to describe the feelings of a naturalist wandering alone in a Brazilian rainforest for the first time. Above all, I admire the sheer luxuriance of the vegetation. Elegant grasses sway gently in the breeze. Parasitic plants, such as orchids and vines, wrap around tree trunks and hang from branches like decorations. Beautiful flowers and glossy leaves reflect the sunlight. For someone who loves nature as much as I do, exploring this rainforest brings a deeper pleasure than I may ever feel again.

Walking through the shady forest, I notice a paradoxical mixture of sound and silence. The buzzing insects are so loud that our sailors even hear them on the ship anchored hundreds of yards from the shore. Yet, deep within the forest, it is silent.

After hours of wandering, I reluctantly turn back toward the ship's landing place. Before I can reach the shore, a tropical storm sweeps over me with sudden force. I seek shelter under a tree with a thick canopy that would easily keep out a common English rain, but here the water pours down the trunk in streams, soaking me completely within minutes.

The violent rain is the reason why the rainforest is green, even on the ground. Unlike in colder climates, where rain often evaporates or is caught by the branches of the trees before it can reach the soil, the heavy tropical showers drench the ground, feeding even the thickest undergrowth.

I will leave a more detailed description of Bahia's gaudy scenery for later, when we return here on our homeward voyage.

San Salvador Geology

All along the coast of Brazil, the solid rock is granite. This granite extends far inland and stretches for at least 2,000 miles. It is curious that such an enormous area could be shaped in this way. Most geologists believe that granite is formed when molten rock crystallizes under great heat and pressure. Did these rocks form beneath a deep ocean? Or were they once buried under other layers of rock that have since worn away? Can we believe that any force, acting for a limited time, can erode granite across such a vast area?

Near the city of San Salvador I notice dark, glossy rocks in a small stream, merely a rivulet of water, flowing into the sea. This coating makes the rocks look polished. The stones, burnished smooth and glittering in the sunlight, are an incredible sight.

The rocks remind me of those described by the influential naturalist Alexander von Humboldt (Humboldt and Bonpland 1821). He writes that the rocks are made of are syenite (a stone similar to granite) at the waterfalls of major rivers like the Orinoco, Nile, and Congo. He also notes they are coated with a thin, shiny black layer. Other scientists, including the chemist Jöns Jacob Berzelius, discovered that this black layer is made of metallic oxides, specifically manganese and iron. Interestingly, the coating only forms on rocks periodically washed by fast-moving water. As the native people of the Orinoco say, "The rocks are black where the waters are white."

Here in Brazil, the coating is a rich brown instead of black, and seems to consist mostly of ferruginous (iron-based) matter. They appear only in areas washed by the tides, where the waves provide a gentle polishing effect similar to that created elsewhere by the rushing waters of great rivers. Here, rising and falling tides likely mimic the seasonal floods of those rivers, producing similar results under different conditions.

The exact origin of these metallic coatings remains unknown. Why are they so thin, yet consistently the same thickness across different regions? No clear explanation has yet been found, but their presence adds another layer of mystery to this area's geology.

Dark stones washed by the river and ocean waters glitter in the sunlight.
Herbert H. Smith, 1879.

Pufferfish

Today I am amused by the behavior of a pufferfish (*Chilomycterus antennatus*) that we catch swimming near the shore. This creature is named for its unique ability to puff itself up into a nearly round, balloon-like shape. Its loose, flabby skin allows it to expand far beyond its normal size.

I take the fish out of the water for a short time, then immerse it again. I watch as it inflates itself by taking in a considerable amount of both air and water. It does this in two ways. First, it swallows air, which it then forces into its body. Muscles keep the air trapped, as you can see from the muscles moving beneath its skin. Second, the fish holds its mouth wide open and motionless, allowing water to gently flow inside. There must be some suction that pulls the water in.

The belly skin is much looser than the skin on the back, thus the abdomen gets far larger than the back. As a result, the fish floats upside-down. Some scientists, like the French zoologist Georges Cuvier, doubt whether a fish could swim in this upside-down position. To my surprise, it not only swims forward in a straight line, but it also turns to either side. It achieves this by using only its pectoral fins (the fins on its sides), while its tail remains collapsed and unused.

After staying puffed up for a while, the fish suddenly deflates, releasing air and water with a powerful spurt through its gills and mouth. It also appears to control how much water it expels, likely adjusting its specific gravity to move through the water more effectively.

Pufferfish (*Chilomycterus antennatus*). Frank Edward Clarke, 1899.

The pufferfish defends itself in several ways. It can give a severe bite and squirt water from its mouth over a surprising distance while making a curious noise by moving its jaws. When inflated, the tiny spines on its skin stick out, making it look like a spiky ball.

The oddest thing about this fish is its ability to secrete a beautiful carmine-red substance from the skin on its belly when handled. I use this to dye ivory and paper, and find that the red color is permanent. In fact, it remains bright even as I am writing this some years later. I do not know the nature or purpose of this secretion.

Dr. Allan of Forres once tells me an incredible story about pufferfish. He finds pufferfish, fully inflated and alive, inside shark stomachs. On many occasions, the pufferfish eats through the stomach wall of the shark and escapes through its side, ultimately killing the much larger predator. Who could imagine that a soft little fish could destroy the great and savage shark?

Hammerhead shark, Rio de Janeiro. Jacques Burkhardt, 1865.

March 18, 1832
Sailing from Bahia—Discolored Water

A few days after we sail from Bahia, while nearing the Abrolhos Islets, I notice an unusual reddish-brown color in the sea. Curious, I examine the water under a magnifying glass and discover that the surface seems to be covered in tiny, jagged bits resembling chopped hay.

These bits are actually minute cylindrical conferva (a type of filamentous algae), bundled into rafts containing 20–60 strands each. These tiny organisms belong to a species called *Trichodesmium erythraeum*, as identified by Miles Joseph Berkeley, a leading British botanist and mycologist. Remarkably, this is the same species found in the Red Sea, and the reason for its name (Montagne 1844b, 1844a).

The sheer number of these conferva is astonishing. As our ship moves through the water, we pass through several dense bands of them. One of these bands is about 10 yards wide and stretches for at least two and a half miles, judging by the muddy, reddish-brown color of the water in the distance.

Sailors and scientists alike have reported conferva in many places during long voyages. For example, René Primevère Lesson, the naturalist aboard the French ship *La Coquille*, describes red water off Lima that was apparently produced by the same cause (Duperrey 1826). Likewise, the distinguished French naturalist François Péron gives us at least twelve references to voyagers who mentioned discolored seawater (Péron 1807). We can add numerous more references to this strange phenomenon, including Humboldt (1821), Flinders (1814), Labillardière (1800), Ulloa (1772), Dumont d'Urville (1830), and Captain King off the coast of Australia (1827). These frequent sightings of vast numbers of microorganisms remind us how even the smallest creatures can have a large effect, even changing the appearance of vast stretches of ocean.

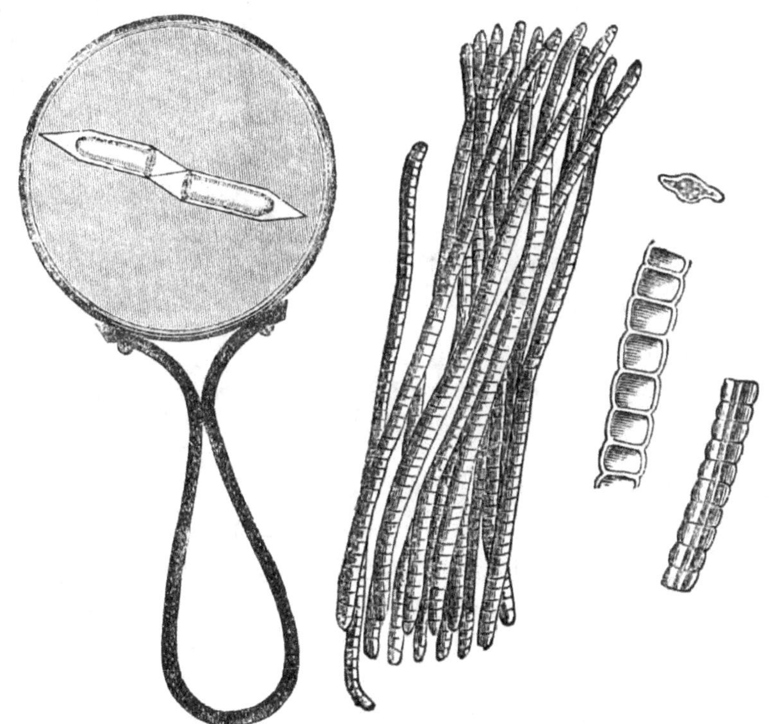

The sea is colored red by algal filaments (*Trichodesmium erythraeum*). Mary Somerville, 1869. Magnified view. Charles Darwin, 1860.

Rio de Janeiro & Excursion North of Cape Frio

April 8, 1832

Shortly after I arrive in Rio de Janeiro, I meet an Englishman who invites me to join him on a journey to visit his estate, located more than 100 miles north of the city, near Cape Frio. I gladly accept his kind offer.

Seven of us ride out as a group on a powerfully hot day. As we ride through the woods, the only movement comes from large, brilliantly colored butterflies, lazily fluttering about. The view from the hills behind Praia Grande is breathtaking. Intense shades of dark blue dominate the scene. The sky and the calm waters of the bay compete with each other in their splendor. After passing through some farmland, we enter the grandest forest imaginable. The towering trees, thick vines, and vibrant green foliage create a natural cathedral that leaves me in awe.

By midday, we reach Itacuruçá, a small village situated on a flat plain. The huts of the black slaves are neatly arranged around the central house, reminding me of drawings of Hottentot villages in Southern Africa.

Brilliantly colored blue morpho and swallowtail butterflies lazily flutter about in Brazil. Marianne North, c. 1873.

Granite Massif in the Moonlight

As the moon rises early this evening, we decide to continue on toward Lagoa de Maricá, where we plan to spend the night. As darkness falls, we ride under a steep-sided granite hill eerily lit by the rising moon. These massive granite hills are common in this region.

This particular hill was once home to runaway slaves. They managed to eke out a subsistence by farming small plots of land near its peak. Eventually, they were discovered and most were

Runaway slaves eke out a subsistence on a hill near Rio de Janeiro. Eduard Hildebrandt, 1846.

captured by soldiers. One elderly woman chose to leap from the summit and be dashed to pieces on the rocks below rather than return to slavery. If this were a story about a woman from ancient Rome, we would call this a noble love of freedom, but for a poor black slave the locals consider it merely beastly stubbornness.

Tonight, we ride for hours along miles of intricate roads that wind through a desert waste of marshes and lagoons. The scene is desolate under the dim light of the moon. A few fireflies flit by us and a solitary snipe cries out plaintively as it rises into the sky. The gloomy roar of the distant sea scarcely breaks the night's stillness.

A snipe plaintively cries out as it rises into the sky. Francois Nicolas Martinet, 1793.

View of distant hills reflected in the calm waters of a large lagoon. Louis Rémy Mignot, 1863.

April 9, 1832

Saltwater Lagoons, Parasitic Plants & Blistering Heat

We leave our miserable shelter before sunrise, traveling along a narrow stretch of flat sand lying between the sea and a series of saltwater lagoons. The sight of many beautiful egrets, cranes, and other fishing birds, as well as fleshy plants growing in fantastical shapes makes the otherwise dull scene interesting. The branches of the few stunted trees are loaded with parasitic plants. I especially admire the beauty and delicious fragrance of the orchids.

The day becomes hotter as the sun rises higher. I find the sunlight and heat reflecting off the white sand very distressing. According to my thermometer, the temperature is 84°F in the shade. When we finally stop for lunch at a local *venda*, we are refreshed by the view of distant wooded hills reflected in the perfectly calm water of an enormous lagoon.

Customs of Hospitality

Whenever a stranger approaches a house here, the inhabitants toll a large bell and often fire small cannons. This loudly announces their arrival to nothing but the rocks and woods.

The houses are usually large, built with thick, upright posts and walls made from plaster over interwoven branches. They stand in a courtyard where they feed the horses. Though they seldom have floors or glass windows, they are generally well-roofed. The front of the building is always an open veranda with tables and benches where guests can sit and eat. Bedrooms are attached to either side. In these rooms, a traveler may sleep as comfortably as he is able on a wooden platform covered with a thin straw mat.

Upon arrival, our custom is to first unsaddle our horses and feed them corn (here they have the native corn, also called maize). Then, we politely bow to the *senhor* (host) and ask him to do us the favor of giving us something to eat.

"Anything you choose, sir," the host usually answers.

At first this seems promising, and I silently thank Providence for guiding us to such a good man. However, as the conversation continues, I learn that the true situation is indeed deplorable.

"Can you do us the favor of giving us any fish?"

"Oh! No, sir."

"Any soup?"

"No, sir."

"Any bread?"

"Oh! No, sir."

"Any dried meat?"

"Oh! No, sir."

If we are lucky, we might get chicken, rice, and *farinha* (cassava powder) after waiting a couple of hours. Sometimes, we even have to catch and kill the chicken with stones ourselves.

A conversation at a roadside *venda*. James Wells Champney, 1879.

Once we are completely exhausted and starving, if we timidly hint that we would be glad to have our dinner, our pompous host answers, "It will be ready when it is ready!" Though true, this response is most unsatisfactory. If we dare to complain we might be told to leave, as they view this sort of impatience as rude.

Most of the hosts are ill-mannered and bad-tempered. They are dirty and their houses are filthy. Homes often lack basic utensils like forks, knives, and spoons. I am sure that these places are more absent of basic comforts than any cottage or hovel in England.

However, at Campos Novos, we eat sumptuously. Here they serve us a feast of rice, chicken, biscuits, wine, and liquor followed by coffee for dinner in the evening. For breakfast, we have fish with coffee. All this costs just $12.50 per person.

Despite this generosity, when one of our group asks about a missing whip, the host gruffly replies, "How should I know? Why didn't you take care of it? I suppose the dogs have eaten it."

Life in the Saltwater Lagoons

After leaving Mangaratiba, we continue our travels, passing through an intricate wilderness of lakes. I find many shells in the lakes. Some shells are from freshwater species, while other shells are from saltwater species. In one lake, I find an abundance of *Lymnaea*, a type of freshwater snail. The locals tell me that the sea flows into this lake at least once a year, turning the water salty. These lagoons, which stretch all along Brazil's coast, likely hold many interesting facts to be discovered about marine and freshwater animals.

Solen (top; d'Orbigny, 1835), *Mytilus* (left; Brown, 1827) and *Pomacea* (right; Swainson, 1822).

The French naturalist Claude Gay previously found both freshwater and saltwater species living together in the brackish waters near Rio, where the fresh and saltwater mix (Gay 1833). Is it unusual that marine species, such as those from the genera *Solen* and *Mytilus*, live alongside freshwater *Pomacea?*

Perhaps not, as I find a *Hydrophilus* water beetle in the salty Rodrigo de Freitas Lagoon near the Botanical Garden in Rio de Janeiro. This lagoon contains only one type of shell from a genus usually found in estuaries where the freshwater from the river meets the saltwater of the ocean.

Orchids & Termite Mounds

Leaving the coastline behind, we reenter the forest. I am astonished by the white trunks of the lofty trees. They are very different from those found in Europe! I write in my notebook, "wonderful and beautiful flowering parasites," as the orchids always strike me as the most novel sight despite the grandness of the scene.

Traveling onward, we cross grassy plains injured by enormous hills made by white ants, also called termites. Some of these conical mounds are nearly 12 feet high. They remind me of Humboldt's sketches of mud volcanoes at Jorullo.

We reach Engenho do Mato after dark, exhausted after ten hours on horseback. I am always surprised at the amount of work that Brazilian horses can do. They also recover from injuries much sooner than English breeds.

Grassy plains damaged by enormous conical termite hills. Anonymous, c. 1884.

April 13, 1832
Sossêgo, Senhor Manuel Figuireda's Estate

After traveling for three days, we reach Sossêgo and stay at the estate of Senhor Manuel Figuireda, a relative of one of our companions. His simple house is shaped like a barn, which is well-suited to the warm climate. The gilded chairs and sofas in the sitting room look odd in contrast with the whitewashed walls, thatched roof, and windows without glass. The house is part of a roughly square arrangement of buildings that includes grain storehouses, stables for the animals, and workshops for the blacks who are taught various trades. In the center of the square, a large pile of coffee beans lies drying in the sun. The buildings stand on a little hill from which I can look out over the cultivated land. Beyond that, we are surrounded on all sides by a dark wall of luxuriant green forest.

Produce of the Plantations

Coffee is the main crop of this region. On average, each tree produces about two pounds of coffee annually, though some yield as much as eight.

The people grow large amounts of *mandioca* (also called cassava). Every part of the plant is useful. The large starchy roots are ground into pulp, pressed, dried, and baked into farinha, the main staple food in Brazil. Horses eat the leaves and stalks. Curiously, the juice of this nutritious plant is highly poisonous, as we see when a cow dies after drinking it at this estate.

Senhor Figuireda proudly shares his impressive yields from the previous year. One bag of *feijões* (beans) produced 80 bags. Three bags of rice yielded a staggering 960 bags. The estate also boasts excellent cattle pasture and forests so rich in wildlife that hunters killed a fresh deer on each of the last three days.

At Mangaratiba, we dine at a very good *venda*. As I have the rare and pleasant memory of an exceptional meal there, I gratefully describe it

Mandioca. Louise van Panhuys, 1816.

here as a representative example of its kind. The abundance of food is evident at dinner, where, if the tables do not groan, the guests certainly do. Everyone is expected to sample every dish. One day, just when I think I have nicely calculated to be sure that nothing was left untasted, I am utterly dismayed when a roast turkey and a whole pig appear in all their substantial reality.

I notice that during our meals a man is employed in driving out old hounds and dozens of little black children, who creep in together at every opportunity.

One morning, I walk out in the darkness an hour before dawn to enjoy the solemn stillness of the scene. After a while, a morning hymn sung in unison by the entire group of blacks breaks the silence. This is how they begin their daily work. On these plantations, I believe that the slaves are happy and content. They work for themselves on Saturdays and Sundays, which is enough to support a man and his family for a full week in this fertile climate. If I could forget for a moment the horror of slavery, I could see the appeal of this simple and patriarchal life that is perfectly removed and independent of the rest of the world.

Slave house surrounded by banana, papaya, and pineapple plants. Johann Moritz Rugendas, 1832.

April 14, 1832
Estate on the Rio Macaé

Today we leave Sossêgo and ride to another estate which is located on the Rio Macaé. This is the last patch of cultivated land we cross in that direction.

The estate is huge, at least two and a half miles long. The owner has forgotten how wide it is. Only a small piece of the land has been cleared, but it looks to me as though nearly every acre is capable of producing the various rich crops of a tropical climate. Considering Brazil's enormous size, the amount of cultivated land seems insignificant compared to the untouched wilderness. In the future, this country will certainly support a vast population!

On the second day of our journey, the road is so overgrown that a man has to go ahead with a sword to cut through the thick creepers. The forest abounds with beauty. I especially admire the tree ferns with their bright green fronds curving elegantly from the tops of their slender trunks.

Extraordinary Evaporation

Heavy rain falls in the evening. Although the thermometer reads 65°F, I feel quite cold. Once the rain stops, I see the most curious sight—the whole forest begins steaming as if releasing columns of smoke. Dense white vapor rises from the trees in the valleys, burying the hills in mist. I observe this extraordinary phenomenon several times during my stay in Brazil. I conclude it is caused by the sun's heat evaporating the moisture from the large surface of the forest's leaves.

Country estate. Frans Post, 1851.

Atrocities of a Slave Country

During my stay at this estate, I nearly witness the kind of atrocious act that can only happen in a country where slavery is allowed. Due to a lawsuit and a quarrel, the owner of the estate planned to sell all the women and children slaves separately from the men at a public auction in Rio. In the end, financial concerns rather than compassion stopped him. Indeed, I believe that the cruelty of separating thirty families who have lived together for many years never crossed his mind. Yet, I would vow that he is a better man than most in humanity and good feeling. Is there no limit to the blindness caused by self-interest and habitual selfishness?

Here I will mention a small story that strikes me with more force than any tale of cruelty. One day, I cross a river on a ferry with a black man who appears especially stupid. In my efforts to make him understand me, I raise my voice and make gestures, accidentally waving my hand close to his face. He must have thought I was angry and about to strike him. Instantly, he looks frightened, half-shuts his eyes, and drops his hands. I will always remember my feelings of surprise, disgust, and shame to see a large and powerful man afraid to defend himself from a blow that he thought was aimed at his face. It shows that years of slavery have taught him to tolerate a degradation lower than what the most helpless animal will abide.

Brazilian slave from Kilwa, East Africa. Johann Rugendas, 1830.

April 18, 1832

Elegant Trees, Creepers & Understory

On our return journey, we spend two more days at Sossêgo where I keep myself busy exploring the nearby forest and collecting insects. Though the trees are very tall, they are surprisingly slender, with trunks only three or four feet around. However, there were a few giants among them. In fact, Senhor Manuel is starting to carve a 70-foot canoe from the solid trunk of a tree that was originally 110 feet long and impressively thick.

The forest is filled with contrasts, and the sight of palm trees growing among the more typical branching trees gives the area a distinctly tropical feel. The açaí palm is one of the most beautiful ornaments of the forest. Its trunk is so slim that I can wrap my two hands around it, but it waves its elegant crown of leaves 40 to 50 feet high into the air.

The forest is also filled with woody vines, called lianas, winding their way up the trees. Some are as thick as two feet around. These lianas are themselves often covered by other vines, creating an intricate web. Some older trees appear especially curious, with curling lianas hanging from their branches like bundles of hay.

When I turn my eye from the world of leaves above to the ground below, I notice the extreme elegance of the ferns and feathery *Mimosa*. In some parts of the forest, the ground is carpeted by *mimosa* plants only a few inches high. As I walk across these thick beds, the sensitive leaves droop, marking the track of my passage.

It is easy to describe my admiration for individual objects in this grand scene, but I cannot adequately convey the feelings of wonder, astonishment, and devotion which fill and lift my mind.

Açaí palm (*Euterpe oleracea*). Anonymous, 1901.

Mimosa pudica. Manuel Blanco, 1800s.

April 19–April 23, 1832
Chirping Sand & Bad Roads

Leaving Sossêgo, we return back the way we came, retracing our steps for the first two days. It is tiring work, as the road runs close to the coast across a glaring, hot, sandy plain. As we travel, I notice that the fine, siliceous sand makes a gentle chirping sound each time my horse presses his hoof into it.

On the third day, we take a different route and pass through the cheerful little village of Madre de Deus. Now we are on one of the principal roads in Brazil, but it is in such a bad state that no wheeled vehicles can pass except the clumsy wagons pulled by oxen. Along the entire journey, I see no stone bridges at all. The wooden bridges made of logs are often so damaged that we have to find ways to go around them.

All distances are inaccurate and nobody seems to know exactly how far it is from one place to another. Instead of milestones, crosses line the road to mark places where human blood has been spilled. On the evening of April 23rd, we finally arrive back in Rio, bringing our pleasant little excursion to an end.

Travelers on the hot, sandy road into Rio de Janeiro. Alfred Martinet, 1852.

Botafogo Bay, Rio de Janeiro

Delightful cottage at Botafogo Bay nestled at the base of Corcovado Mountain.
William Gore Ouseley, 1852.

April 24–July 5, 1832

During the remainder of my stay in Rio, I have the pleasure of living in a small cottage at Botafogo Bay. The beauty of the scenery around Botafogo Bay is famous and I could not wish for anything more delightful than spending a few weeks in such a magnificent country.

In England, anyone who loves nature also enjoys walking because there is always something interesting to see. But here the fertile tropics are so teeming with life and there are so many attractions that I can scarcely walk at all.

The cottage where I live is nestled at the base of the majestic Corcovado Mountain. The dramatic, conical hills in this area are characteristic of a type of ancient rock formation that the scientist Humboldt describes as gneiss-granite. Nothing is more impressive than the view of these huge rounded masses of naked rock rising sharply from a sea of luxuriant, green vegetation.

Terrestrial Planarians

During my time in the forest, I mostly focus my observations on invertebrate animals, those without backbones. I am particularly fascinated by a type of planarian that lives on dry land. Planarians, or flatworms, are simple animals with remarkable regenerative powers. The structure of these creatures is so basic that

Land planarian with colorful stripes. Max Weber, 1890.

Cuvier classified them with parasitic intestinal worms, even though they are never found inside other animals. While many planarian species live in saltwater or freshwater, those I find here live in the forest, even in dry places where they stay hidden under the rotten wood on which they feed.

Their structure is simple. They are shaped like narrow little slugs. Some have beautifully colored stripes running lengthwise along their bodies. They have two small slits on their undersides. A sensitive, funnel-shaped mouth protrudes from the front slit. Remarkably, this mouth continues moving long after the animal itself dies.

Out of curiosity, I experiment with their famous ability to regenerate. I carefully cut one into two nearly equal parts. One half has both of the slits on the bottom, while the other half has none. Within two weeks, both halves are shaped like whole animals. Within 25 days, the half with a mouth and other organs has fully regrown into a normal planarian. The other half began to form a rudimentary cup-shaped mouth. Unfortunately, the mouth has not yet opened when the intense heat kills all my specimens as we approach the equator, though I am certain it would have completely regenerated its structure. Although this experiment is well-known, it is interesting to watch with my own eyes as the animals gradually produce every essential organ from only the tips of their bodies.

I discovered twelve different species of terrestrial planarians over the course of my travels in the southern hemisphere. Some specimens that I collect on the Island of Tasmania I keep alive for nearly two months, feeding them on rotting wood. I bring many specimens back to England, though I find preserving planarians incredibly difficult. Once they die, their bodies rapidly dissolve into liquid—a process I have never seen happen so quickly in any other animal.

Hunting in the Rainforest

My first visit to the forest where I find the planarians is on a hunting trip with an old Portuguese priest. He hunts by releasing a few dogs into the forest and then patiently waiting to shoot at any animal that appears. The son of a nearby farmer joins us. He is a wild Brazilian youth dressed in a tattered shirt and trousers with no hat, carrying an old-fashioned gun and a large knife.

Everyone carries a knife in Brazil. It is almost always needed to cut through the thick forest vines. This custom is also partly responsible for the frequent murders. The Brazilians are so dexterous with their knives that they can throw them with precision and fatal force. I once watch little boys play a game where they practice throwing knives at upright sticks, demonstrating impressive skill. Doubtless their abilities will improve and may be used for more serious ends in the future.

The day before my visit my companion shot two large bearded monkeys (*Sapajus libidinosus*). These monkeys have prehensile tails that can grip and support their entire weight, even after death. Another monkey we kill remains hanging from a branch by its tail. We have to cut down the large tree to retrieve it. The tree and monkey come down together in an awful crash. Our day of hunting brings us little else besides the monkey, a few small green parrots, and some toucans. But my acquaintance with the priest proves valuable on another occasion when he gives me a fine specimen of the jaguarundi, a wild cat native to the Americas.

Jaguarundi (*Puma yagouaroundi*). Richard Lydekker, 1896.

Clouds on the Corcovado

One of my favorite activities while at Botafogo Bay is watching the clouds roll in from the sea and gather just beneath the peak of Corcovado Mountain. When partly veiled in this manner, the mountain appears far higher than its real height of 2,300 feet.

John Frederic Daniell's meteorological essays state that clouds sometimes appear stuck on a mountaintop, even as the wind blows over them. On Corcovado, I observe something slightly different. The clouds curl over the summit and continue drifting past, yet they stay the same size.

I believe that the explanation lies in the interaction between warm and cool air. As the sun sets in the evening, a gentle breeze strikes the southern face of the mountain. The warm air rises to the top of the mountain. There it mingles with cooler air, causing its moisture to condense into clouds. However, as the light wreaths of clouds cross the mountain top and contact the warmer air on the northern slope, the moisture in the air immediately dissolves again.

Clouds gathered around Corcovado Mountain.
William Lionel Wyllie, 1914.

Hyla frogs perform every evening. George Albert Boulenger, 1898.

Heavy Rain & Musical Frogs

The climate is delightful during the start of winter in this region (May–June). I measure the temperature every day at 9 o'clock in the morning and evening, and calculate that the average temperature is a comfortable 72°F.

Heavy rainstorms are common, but the dry winds blowing from the south make my walks pleasant despite the rain. One morning, more than one and a half inches of rain falls in just six hours. The sound of raindrops hitting the countless leaves in the Corcovado forest can be heard from a distance of a quarter of a mile away; it sounds like the rushing of a great body of water. After particularly hot days, it is delicious to sit quietly in the garden, watching the evening fade into night.

In the tropics, nature's top vocalists are humbler performers than in Europe. Here, a tiny *Hyla* frog sits on a blade of grass just above the water and chirps pleasantly. When several frogs are together, they sing different notes in harmony. Cicadas and crickets join in the evening song. Though their cry is constant and shrill, at a distance it softens into a pleasant background melody. This great concert begins every evening after dark. I often sit listening to it until some curious insect draws my attention away.

These frogs are difficult to catch. The ends of their toes have small suckers, allowing them to climb smooth surfaces, even a vertical pane of glass.

Firefly (*Photuris versicolor*). W. H. Lizars, 1852.

Springing beetle (*Ignelater luminosus*). W. H. Lizars, 1852.

Bioluminescent Insects

In the evenings I watch fireflies flitting about the hedges. On the darkest nights, their glowing lights are visible as far as 200 paces away. It is remarkable that all the glowing creatures I have ever observed emit green light. This includes fireflies, glowworms, and marine animals like jellyfish, *Clytia*, polychaete worms (Nereididae), and *Pyrosoma*. The fireflies here are part of the Lampyridae family, the same family as the English glowworm. Most of the ones I catch belong to a species called *Photuris versicolor*.

These fireflies flash most brilliantly when irritated. Between flashes, the two glowing rings on their abdomens go dark. The two rings flash at almost the same time, but I see that the flash starts sooner in the front ring. The substance that makes the fireflies shine is a sticky fluid. Little spots where I tear the skin continue to shine brightly, while the rest of the body remains dark. When I remove the head, the decapitated body continues to shine and scintillate, although less intensely. The brightness always increases when I poke the rings with a needle. In one case, the insect remains lit for nearly 24 hours after its death. From this fact, I infer that the animal makes an effort to conceal its light, while shining is involuntary.

I find many larvae of these fireflies on the damp gravel paths. Their shape is similar to the female of the English species. Unlike the adults, the larvae glow only feebly. They pretend to be dead and stop shining when I touch them.

I capture several larvae and keep them alive to observe them. Their tails are interesting, serving both as suction cups to help them attach to surfaces and as reservoirs for fluid. When I feed the larvae raw meat, I see that they always bring the tips of their tails to their mouths before exuding a drop of fluid onto the meat. The process is clumsy—despite practice, their tails often miss their mouths and have to first touch the neck as a guide.

Springing Beetles

The most common luminous insect I find in Bahia is a beetle called *Ignelater luminosus*. Its light also becomes brighter when irritated.

I amuse myself one day watching this insect springing into the air—an ability that was not well-described by previous writers. When placed on its back, the beetle prepares to spring by tilting its head and thorax (the insect's chest) backward. The beetle uses its muscles to bend its spine back like a spring, until it is balanced on the top of its head and the tips of its wing-cases. When it suddenly relaxes, the head flies up, causing the back to strike the ground with such force that the insect jerks up 1–2 inches into the air. The pointed thorax steadies the body while the insect springs up. The elasticity of the spine does not receive enough emphasis in the descriptions I have read. Such a sudden spring cannot be done only through muscular contraction, it must involve some mechanical mechanism.

Tropical Fruit Trees

During my time in Bahia, I take several short but pleasant excursions into the countryside. One memorable visit is to the Botanical Garden in Rio, where I smell and see many useful plants. I particularly enjoy the delightfully aromatic leaves of camphor, pepper, cinnamon, and clove trees. As for beauty, the breadfruit, jackfruit (here called *jaca*), and mango trees compete in the magnificence of their foliage.

Jackfruit and mango trees shape the character of the landscape around Bahia. Before seeing them, I had no idea that any tree could cast so black a shade on the ground. The dark green of these trees stands out against the bright vegetation here much like the evergreen laurels and hollies contrast with lighter deciduous trees in England.

I see that homes in the tropics are often surrounded by plants that are at once lovely and useful. Bananas, coconut palms, oranges, and breadfruit trees provide both beauty and food. Who could doubt the harmony of usefulness and elegance in these tropical treasures?

Breadfruit trees cast deep shade in the tropics. John Tyley, 1800.

Blue Haze

On the same day that I visit the Botanical Garden, I am struck by something said by the naturalist Humboldt. He often describes the "thin vapour" that softens and blends colors to be more harmonious without obscuring the air's clarity. I have never seen this effect in temperate regions. But here, landscapes viewed at half a mile away are perfectly lucid, but at a greater distance all the colors blend into a beautiful haze of soft French grey tinted with blue. I later learn that this effect is linked to the dryness of the morning air.

Topsail Mountain

Another morning, I set out early to climb the Pedra da Gávea, or Topsail Mountain. The cool air smells delightfully fragrant. Shimmering dew drops cling to the broad leaves of lilies shading the small streams of clear water. I sit on a granite boulder and delightedly watch insects and birds fly past. Hummingbirds seem particularly fond of this hidden, shady spot. When I watch them buzzing round a flower, with wings vibrating too rapidly for the eye to see, I am always reminded of the sphinx moths who have similar behavior.

Following a pathway, I enter a noble forest. At about 500 feet elevation, I enjoy one of those splendid views so common in Rio. At this height, the colors are at their most brilliant. The scene reminds me of the gaudiest sets of a grand opera or theater, though every shape and color completely surpasses anything I have ever seen in Europe. I am overwhelmed with emotion as I view the magnificence all around me.

Botafogo beach—a blue haze blends the colors of the distant hills to a soft French grey. Antônio Parreiras, 1886.

Phallus Fungus

Every time I go out on an excursion I come back with something interesting. One day, I collect a specimen of a strange fungus in the *Phallus* genus. Many people know the English *Phallus*, which emits a foul smell in autumn. However, entomologists, who study insects, know that this odious odor is a delightful fragrance to some beetles. It is the same here. As I carry the fungus, a rove beetle lands on it, drawn by the smell. Entomologists later classify the beetle I collect as *Darwinilus sedarisi*, a new genus named in honor of my discovery.

Though the plants and insects in Brazil are different from those in England, they share similar relationships. Interestingly, when humans introduce new species, these relationships often break down. For example, cabbage and lettuce, which are heavily targeted by slugs and caterpillars in England, remain untouched in Rio's gardens.

The *Phallus* fungus gives off a foul smell that attracts a new beetle species. José Joaquim Freire, 1700s.

Entomology Observations in Brazil

I collect a large variety of insects during my stay in Brazil. It might interest entomologists that the commonness of different insect groups is sometimes quite different to what we find in England.

The brilliant and large butterflies (Lepidoptera order) of this region represent the tropics better than any other animals. This is true only for butterflies. The moths, unexpectedly given the lush vegetation, are less abundant than in temperate regions.

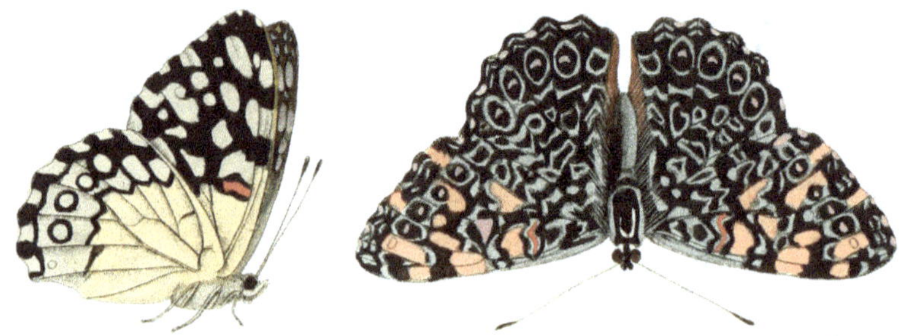

Hamadryas feronia, a butterfly with surprising behavior. Dru Drury, 1770.

Noise Made by a Butterfly

One butterfly, called *Hamadryas feronia*, surprises me with its unusual behavior. This common species is often found flying high in orange groves. It has a peculiar way of perching on tree trunks: it always positions its head downward and keeps its wings spread out horizontally, rather than folding them vertically as most butterflies do. What is more remarkable, this is the only butterfly I have ever seen use its legs to run. Not knowing this at first, it escaped me several times by shuffling sideways just as I was about to catch it with my forceps.

The most unusual feature of this butterfly is its ability to make a noise. When observing mating pairs of these butterflies chasing each other, I distinctly hear a clicking sound, like a gear wheel catching under a spring. I hear the sound repeatedly and as far as 20 yards away. Though it may be hard to believe, I am certain of what I heard.

I later learn that this noise is caused by a peculiar structure in the butterfly's wings. Edward Doubleday presented this information in a paper at the Entomological Society (Doubleday 1845). I also find an account from the Russian explorer Georg von Langsdorff's earlier travels in 1803–7 of a different butterfly, probably *Historis acheronta*, that makes a noise like a rattle.

Beetles

I am disappointed by the beetles (Coleoptera order) in Brazil. There are many, but they are small and dull-colored, unlike the large specimens often displayed in European collections from the tropics. To give an idea of the sheer diversity, I collect 68 beetle species in one day (June 23). On this day, I do not give special attention to this group, as proven by also collecting 37 spider species (Arachnida class). There are so many species here that the thought of the eventual size of a complete catalog is rather unsettling to the mind of a thoughtful naturalist.

The carnivorous beetles (Carabidae family) are surprisingly rare in the tropics, which is a striking contrast to the number of carnivorous four-footed animals in these regions. The scavenger beetles that feed on dead animals, such as those in the Staphylinidae family, are also uncommon. Can this be explained by the many spiders and species in the Hymenoptera order (stinging insects like bees, wasps, and ants) taking over the role of beetle predators?

On the other hand, beetles that feed on plants are astonishingly abundant. In particular, I find many weevils in the Rhynchophorus family and leaf beetles in the Chrysomelidae family. Rather than the diversity of species, it is the sheer number of individual beetles that stands out. Other insects that feed on plants, such as the grasshoppers (Orthoptera order) and the true bugs (Hemiptera order), are also exceptionally numerous.

Beetles in the *Curculio* genus—the sheer number of beetle species in Brazil is rather unsettling to the mind of a thoughtful naturalist. W. H. Lizars, 1852.

Ants

Except for the bees, the stinging insects are abundant (order Hymenoptera, which includes wasps and ants).

Army ant (*Eciton burchellii*). Nathalie Escure, 2003.

Upon first entering the tropical forest, I am astonished by the work done by the ants. Well-beaten paths branch off in every direction. A line of foraging ants carrying pieces of green leaves, some larger than their own bodies, is constantly coming and going along the paths.

One day, I notice many spiders, cockroaches, other insects, and some lizards rushing about in a panic across a bit of bare ground. Just behind them, a swarm of small ants advances behind them in such great numbers that they entirely cover and blacken every stalk of grass and every leaf. The swarm of ants crosses the bare ground, divides into two lines, and comes down an old wall. By this means they surround many insects. The poor little creatures make impressive efforts to extricate themselves from this death trap.

When the ants reach the road, they change course and go back up the wall in narrow lines. When I place a small stone in the way of one of the lines, they all attack it, and then retreat. Soon after, they charge to attack the stone again. Failing again, they entirely give up that route. They could have easily gone around the little stone, and doubtless they would have if it were there all along. But as it had attacked them, the lion-hearted little warriors refused to yield.

Leafcutter ants: 1) minor worker, 2) major worker, 3) subterranean worker. E. W. Robinson, 1863.

Wasp Killing a Spider

In Rio de Janeiro I often see wasp nests built from clay in the veranda corners. The little wasps stuff their nest cells full of half-dead spiders and caterpillars. It is wondrous that they seem to know exactly how much venom to inject to leave their prey paralyzed but alive until the wasp eggs hatch and the larvae feed on their horrified, powerless victims. One enthusiastic naturalist described this sight as curious and pleasing!

Another day, I am fascinated by watching a deadly battle between a wasp in the *Pepsis* genus and a large spider in the *Lycosa* genus. To begin, the wasp suddenly attacks the spider, and then flies away. The spider, obviously wounded, tries to escape but only manages to roll down a little hill. It barely has the strength to crawl into a thick tuft of grass to hide. The wasp quickly returns, surprised that its victim is gone. It then starts to hunt as methodically as a hound after a fox. It circles round, rapidly vibrating its wings and antennae. Despite the spider's clever hiding spot, the wasp soon locates it. The wasp is apparently still afraid of the spider's jaws, because it maneuvers carefully around before stinging the spider twice more on the underside of its body. At last, carefully checking the motionless spider with its antennae to be sure it is paralyzed, it begins to drag the body away. But I stop both predator and prey.

Don Félix de Azara, the renowned Spanish military officer and naturalist, tells the story of a wasp, probably also in the *Pepsis* genus, dragging a dead spider through tall grass to its nest 163 paces away! He notes that the wasp stopped from time to time to make small half circles to stay on course (Azara 1809).

Wasps attacking large bird spiders. Edward Step, 1916.

Golden Web Weaving Spider & Parasite

Here in Brazil, there are far more spiders, relative to other invertebrates, than I find in England. This difference is probably greater among these species than with any other kind of animal. The jumping spiders alone appear to have an almost infinite diversity of species. They have an extraordinary variety of shapes. For example, some species have leathery pointed shells while others have long spiny legs.

Every forest path is barricaded by the strong yellow webs of the spider *Leucauge argyrobapta*. The important collector from the 1600s, Hans Sloane, says that a closely related species in the Caribbean, *Trichonephila clavipes*, makes webs strong enough to catch birds! When I look closely, I notice that there is a small spider with long front legs that lives as a parasite on almost all of these enormous webs. This small spider seems to belong to an undescribed genus. I suppose it is too insignificant for the great orb-weaver spider to notice. Therefore, the larger spider allows it to prey on the smaller insects caught on the lines of the web that would otherwise go to waste. When this little spider is frightened, it either plays dead by extending its front legs or suddenly drops from the web.

Brazilian orb-weaver spiders exhibit an extraordinary variety of shapes (from left: *Gasteracantha cancriformis*, *Micrathena furcata*, and *Acrosomoides acrosomoides*). Ernst Haeckel, 1904.

Spider Tricks

One colorful spider reinforces its large web by two or four zigzag ribbons near the center. It is especially common in dry areas where it builds its web in the huge leaves of the common agave. Later entomologists identify it as *Argiope argentata*, which is related to *Glyptogona sextuberculata* and *Cyclosa conica*. Oddly, this spider always stands at the center of its web, head down.

When a large insect is caught, such as a wasp or grasshopper, the spider spins it rapidly, encasing it in threads until it resembles a silkworm cocoon. The spider then examines the powerless victim and delivers a fatal bite to the back of the thorax, retreating until the venom takes effect. This venom is highly potent. As evidence of this, I once opened a cocoon to find that a large wasp was dead within half a minute.

When I disturb the spider, its response varies depending on the situation. If there are bushes below, it suddenly drops from the web. I distinctly see the animal releasing thread to prepare for its fall. If the ground is clear below it, it seldom falls. Instead, it quickly runs to the other side of the web. When I disturb it more, it does something quite curious: it violently jerks its web until the whole thing vibrates so rapidly that the spider becomes blurred and almost invisible.

These spiders remind me of a time in England when I watch a determined little spider feeding on much larger prey. It is well known that most British spiders will cut the strands of their web to free a large insect caught in it, saving the web from being completely destroyed. However, in a hothouse in Shropshire, I once see a small spider catch a large female wasp in its asymmetrical web. Rather than cutting the web, the spider persistently works to further entangle the wasp's body, focusing especially on its wings. At first, the trapped wasp repeatedly tries to sting the spider, but misses every time. After watching the wasp struggle for over an hour, I begin to feel pity for it. I remove it from the web, kill it, and then place it back onto the web. The spider quickly returns. An hour later, to my great surprise, I see its jaws buried in the hole where the wasp's stinger emerges when it is alive. Although I drive the spider away two or three times, it keeps returning over the next 24 hours to feed from the same spot, growing visibly swollen from the juices of its much larger prey.

South American rhea (*Rhea americana*). Anonymous, 1898.

CHAPTER 3
URUGUAY

Map charting the third stage of the voyage of the *Beagle*, around the Río de la Plata region in Uruguay and down to the Río Negro. Robert FitzRoy, 1839.

A great pod of dolphins furrows the sea as they jump together in graceful arcs. J. Carter Beard, 1914.

July 5, 1832
At Sea From Brazil to Río de la Plata

In the morning we sail out of the splendid harbor of Rio de Janeiro. As we sail south along the coast toward the Río de la Plata (Plata River), we see nothing special except for the extraordinary spectacle of a great pod of dolphins. They cut through the water, furrowing the sea as hundreds jump together in graceful arcs, exposing their entire bodies. Even as the ship speeds along at nine knots (more than ten miles an hour), these animals effortlessly cross and recross in front of the ship's bow and then dash far ahead.

The weather shifts as soon as we enter the wide Río de la Plata, and I begin to observe many novel sights and sounds. One particularly dark night, seals and penguins surround the ship, filling the air with such strange noises that the officer on watch reports he can hear cattle bellowing on the shore! The sea is luminous, glowing from countless tiny bioluminescent creatures. The penguins leave fiery trails in the water as they swim past. On another night, we witness a splendid display of St. Elmo's Fire—a glowing light caused by electrical charges in the air. It is so bright that I can see the wind vane on top of the mast outlined as if it had been rubbed with shining phosphorus. Above, vivid lightning illuminates the dark sky.

As we sail deeper inside the mouth of the river, I am fascinated by watching how slowly the waters of the sea and the Plata River mix. The muddy, discolored freshwater of the river, being less dense, floats atop the saltwater of the sea. This is oddly displayed in the ship's wake, where a line of blue seawater mingles with the muddy river water in little eddies, blue and brown water swirling together behind the ship.

St. Elmo's Fire lights up the mast of the ship on a dark night. G. Hartwig, 1886.

Montevideo & Maldonado

Ship at anchor off Montevideo, the capital city of Uruguay, which became an independent country in 1828. Adolphe d'Hastrel, 1840.

July 26, 1832

Today we anchor at Montevideo, the capital city of the newly independent country of Uruguay, formerly called the Banda Oriental. The *Beagle* will spend the next two years surveying south of the Río de la Plata, mapping all along the eastern and extreme southern coasts of America. To avoid unnecessary repetition, I will share key parts of my journal organized by region, not necessarily in the order we visit them.

Maldonado

This quiet, lonely little town is located on the northern bank of the Río de la Plata, close to the estuary where the river meets the ocean. Like all towns in these countries, it is built with a regular grid of streets running at right angles to each other. The large plaza in the center of the town only makes the scantiness of the population more obvious, as too few people live there to fill the square. Maldonado has hardly any trade. The main exports are hides and live cattle. Most of the people who live here are landowners, along with a few shopkeepers and essential tradesmen, such as blacksmiths and carpenters, who handle nearly all the business within a 50-mile radius.

A mile of sand dunes separates the town and the river. Open, rolling countryside surrounds the town on all other sides. Countless herds of cattle, sheep, and horses graze on the fine, even green grass. I see very little land planted in crops, even close to the town. Only a few cacti and agave hedges mark the places where wheat or corn grows.

The whole northern bank of the Río de la Plata looks similar. The only difference near Maldonado is that the granite hills are slightly higher. I find the scenery rather boring. There are scarcely any houses, enclosures, or even a single tree to cheer up the landscape. Yet, after being imprisoned for so long on the ship, walking over the boundless plains of grass gives me a charming feeling of freedom.

If you look closely, many objects are quite beautiful. Many of the small birds are brilliantly colored and dwarf flowers ornament the bright green pasture where the cattle graze. Among these little flowers, I spot a plant that looks like a daisy, which feels like seeing an old friend.

What would a florist from England say to see entire tracts of land so thickly covered by *Verbena peruviana* that they are a gaudy scarlet when see from a distance?

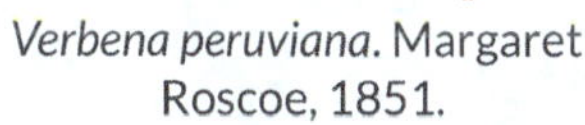

Verbena peruviana. Margaret Roscoe, 1851.

A few cacti and agave mark the edges of fields by Maldonado. Nicanor Blanes, 1889.

Excursion to the Arroyo Polanco

Here I will tell the story of the little excursion I made to the stream called Arroyo Polanco, about seventy miles north of Maldonado. As proof of how cheap things are in this country, I will mention that I only pay $40 a day for two men and a group of about a dozen riding horses.

Before we depart for the journey, my companions arm themselves well with pistols and sabers. At first, I believe their caution is unnecessary. That is until we hear the news that a traveler from Montevideo was found dead the day before, his throat cut near a roadside cross marking the site of an earlier murder.

On the first night, we sleep in a remote country house. Here I learn that I possess some items that astonish the locals. My pocket compass is especially fascinating to them. At every house we visit, they ask me to show them how I use the compass and a map to point the direction to nearby places. They are astonished that a stranger could know the road (in this country, "road" simply means direction) to places I have never been. At one house, a young woman who is ill in bed begs for me to come show her the compass. My surprise is even greater than theirs to find such a lack of knowledge among people who possess thousands of cattle and enormous estates. The only explanation can be that they rarely meet foreigners in their remote location.

A box of wooden matches that I can ignite by biting also causes a stir. People are so amazed that a man can start a fire with his teeth

Ride through the provinces of the Río de la Plata. William MacCann, 1853.

that whole families gather to watch it. Once a local even offers me $20 for a single match!

They ask me many amusing questions, such as whether the earth or the sun moves, whether it is hotter or colder in the north, and where Spain is located. The majority of the people have a vague idea that England, London, and North America are just different names for the same place. Those who are better informed are certain that London and North America are separate countries located near each other and that England is a large town in London!

It is customary in this country to ask for lodging at any convenient house. The astonishment inspired by my compass and other entertaining tricks works to my advantage. My guides share long stories of my curious activities, such as breaking stones, knowing the difference between venomous and harmless snakes, collecting insects, and more. These tales repay my hosts for their hospitality.

I realize now that I write as though I am among the people of central Africa. Though this comparison is not flattering for the people of this South American region, it is how I feel when I am here.

Las Minas

On the second day we ride to the village of Las Minas. The landscape has more hills, but otherwise looks much the same. I imagine that an inhabitant of the flat Pampas might consider these low hills similar to the Alps mountains. We scarcely meet another person all day in this thinly populated country.

Las Minas is a much smaller village than Maldonado. It sits on a little plain, surrounded by low, rocky mountains. Like many towns in the region, it is laid out in a symmetrical grid. The whitewashed church at its center makes it look quite pretty. However, the isolated houses

A local eyes me suspiciously when he sees me washing my face in the morning. Guillermo Facio, 1900s.

outside the village rise from the ground like lonely ghosts, without gardens or courtyards. This is typical of this country and gives the houses an uncomfortable feel.

Washing my face in the morning leads to much speculation in the village of Las Minas. A local tradesman eyes me suspiciously.

Clearly intrigued, he asks me many questions about why I do it. He also asks why men on our ship wear beards, something he heard about from my guide. Perhaps he has heard of ablutions (religious washing) in the Muslim faith, and as he knows I am a heretic because my religion differs from his, he probably concludes that I am therefore also a Turk!

Gaucho with brightly colored garments and knife stuck in his belt like a dagger. Juan Manuel Blanes, 1865.

Gauchos & Rheas

Tonight, we go to a *pulpería*, or drinking shop. Many *gauchos* come in during the evening to drink liquor and smoke cigars. Their appearance is striking. They are usually tall and handsome, but their faces have arrogant and dissolute expressions, as do men who are frequently drunk. They often wear mustaches and their long black hair curls down their backs. Their brightly colored garments, large spurs clanking at their heels, and knives stuck into their belts like daggers make them look like a separate race of men. These *gauchos* look very different from what I expected from the name, which means a simple countryman. The *gauchos* are excessively polite. They never drink without first offering you a taste. While they bow gracefully, they seem equally ready to cut your throat.

On the third day of our excursion north of Maldonado, we ramble along a meandering path because I am busy examining some beds of marble. Along the way, we spot flocks of twenty or thirty rheas (*Rhea americana*) foraging on the bright green grass. These tall birds look similar to ostriches. When standing on a little hill, silhouetted against the clear blue sky, they appear quite noble. In this part of the country, rheas are more tame than anywhere else. We can gallop quite close to them before they flee. They run with wings outstretched like sails in the wind, quickly leaving our horses behind.

South American rhea (*Rhea americana*). Anonymous, 1898.

Half-wild cattle know the danger of the *lazo* and lead the *gauchos* on a long and tiring chase. Emeric Essex Vidal, 1829.

A Visit to Don Juan Fuentes

Tonight we reach the home of Don Juan Fuentes, a wealthy landowner. As my companions and I do not know him personally, we follow the proper etiquette for approaching a stranger's home in this region. First, you ride slowly up to the door and call out, "*Ave Maria*". Then you remain on horseback until someone comes out to ask you to dismount. The owner responds formally, "*Sin pecado concebida*," that is, "Conceived without sin." After entering the house, you must keep up a few minutes of polite conversation before asking permission to stay the night. They always grant it, of course.

Though strangers, we take our meals with the family. They give us rooms in which we make our beds from our saddle blankets (here called *recados*), the same we use when riding our horses, as is typical in the Pampas.

It is curious that people living in similar circumstances have similar customs. I later observe nearly the same customs and hospitality at the Cape of Good Hope in South Africa. However, the people of the two regions have different characters which are shown in the slight differences in customs. The Spaniard of the Pampas asks no personal questions beyond polite conversation, while the Dutch Boer demands to know where you have been, where you are going, your business, and even how many brothers, sisters, or children you have!

Shortly after arriving at Don Juan's, I watch as the *gauchos* drive a large herd of cattle toward the house and pick out three beasts to slaughter. These half-wild cattle are fast. They know full well the danger of the *lazo* (lasso) and lead the horses on a long and tiring chase.

It is quite curious that Don Juan's house is so miserable despite the wealth displayed by the vast herds of cattle, horses, and men. The floor is hardened mud, the windows lack glass, and the sitting room holds only a few rough chairs, stools, and tables. Supper, even with several guests present, consists of two huge piles of meat—one roasted and the other boiled—alongside a few pieces of pumpkin. There are no other vegetables, no bread, and only a single large earthenware jug of water to serve the entire group. Yet Don Juan owns miles of fertile land which would, with a little effort, produce grain and vegetables.

We spend a pleasant evening smoking while the *gauchos* sing and play a guitar. The señoritas (young women) all sit together and dine apart from the men.

Lazos & Bolas

So many books have already described *lazos* and *bolas* that it is hardly worth writing more about them. A *lazo* is a strong, thin rope made of tightly-braided strips of cattle hide with a small ring on one end made from iron or brass. The *gaucho* passes the rope through the ring to form a noose, then attaches the other end to his surcingle (the broad strap that goes around the belly of a horse to secure the saddle). When he wants to use his *lazo*, the *gaucho* holds a small coil of it in the same hand he uses to hold the horse's bridle while he spins the noose around his head with in his other hand. His quick and dexterous wrist movements keep the noose open to about eight feet wide until he is ready to throw it. The noose always lands exactly where he aims. When not using it, he ties his *lazo* in a small coil behind his saddle.

The *bolas*, or balls, are connected by thin braided leather cords. There are two types of *bolas* with different uses. One type is used mainly for catching rheas. It has two balls joined by a single cord about eight feet long. The other type has three balls joined by three cords at a common center. The *gaucho* holds the smallest of the

Gaucho and *lazo*. Juan Manuel Blanes, 1865.

three balls in his hand while whirling the others overhead. When thrown, the balls fly through the air like a shot, hit the target, and tightly wind around it.

The weight and size of the *bolas* vary depending on their purpose. For example, I see lightweight wooden balls the size of a turnip used to catch animals without harming them. Heavier stone, or even iron balls, can be thrown further and with enough force to break a horse's leg.

As I discover, the hardest part about using *bolas* is riding your horse well enough to gallop at full speed, then suddenly turn around while whirling the *bolas* around your head, take aim and throw them. On foot, it is quickly learned.

One day, I amuse myself by whirling the balls around my head while galloping across the plains, until one accidentally hits a bush. This stops the spinning motion, and the *bolas* fall to the ground, magically wrapping around one of my horse's hind legs. Then the second ball jerks out of my hand, and my horse is completely stuck! Luckily, the horse is old and experienced enough to know what happened. Otherwise, he might have panicked and kicked or thrown himself down—and taken me with him. Roaring with laughter, the *gauchos* shout that they have seen every kind of animal caught by the *bolas*, but have never seen a man catch himself!

Partridges

Everywhere we look we see large numbers of partridges (*Nothura maculosa*). They look like very silly birds. They do not travel in coveys (the word for a flock of partridges), nor do they hide when approached like the English kind do. A man on horseback can ride round and round them in a spiral, approaching closer with each turn, and get close enough to knock as many as he wants on the head.

The most common way to catch partridges here is with a type of small *lazo* made from the stem of a rhea feather that is attached to the end of a long stick. A boy riding a quiet, old horse can catch thirty or forty partridges in a single day using this method.

I am reminded of a similar hunting technique used by the people who live in the Arctic part of North America. According to Samuel Hearne's book about his travels there, natives catch snowshoe hares by walking in a spiral around them while they rest on their forms (the shallow holes they make on the ground to hide). The hunters prefer the middle of the day, when the sun is high, and their shadows are shorter, making it harder for the hare to spot them (Hearne 1795).

The silly-looking partridges (*Nothura maculosa*) are unafraid of humans and easy to catch. Anonymous, 1800s.

Sierra de las Ánimas

Over the next two days, I reach the furthest point I want to explore. The landscape looks the same everywhere. After a while, I find the fine green pasture just as tiring as a dusty turnpike road back home in England.

On our way back to Maldonado, we follow a slightly different route. We pass near Pan de Azúcar, a large hill that is a familiar landmark to anyone who has sailed up the Plata River. Here, a hospitable old Spaniard shares his home with me for a day.

Together with the old Spaniard, we climb the Sierra de las Ánimas early in the morning. By the light of the rising sun, the scenery looks almost like a painting. We have expansive views from the top of the mountain. To the west, we can see across the immense flat plain as far as Montevideo. To the east, we look out over the gently rounded hills of Maldonado.

At the mountain's summit, we find several small piles of stones that have clearly lain here for many years. My companion explains that these were made by native people in the old time. The piles resemble smaller versions of the stone cairns often found on the mountains of Wales. It seems that marking significant events on the highest nearby point is a universal human desire. Today, no natives remain in this part of the province. As far as I know, these insignificant stone piles on the summit of the Sierra de las Ánimas are the only permanent record that the former inhabitants left behind.

View over treeless plains looking towards Montevideo. Conrad Martens, 1832.

Absence of Trees

It is remarkable that trees are almost completely absent in this region. Thickets partially cover some of the rocky hills, and I commonly see willows growing along the banks of larger streams in the areas north of Las Minas. I also hear of a forest of palms near the Arroyo Tapes, and see one large palm tree near Pan de Azúcar, at a latitude of 35°. Except for these examples and the trees planted by Spaniards, the region has very little woodland. Among the introduced species are poplars, olives, peaches, and other fruit trees. Peach trees, in fact, grow so successfully that they are the main source of firewood for the city of Buenos Aires.

It appears that trees rarely thrive in very flat areas like the Pampas. At first, I think that perhaps this is due to strong winds or lack of water from excessive drainage robbing the soil of moisture. But in the area around Maldonado, neither of these reasons can explain why there are so few trees. The rocky mountains provide protected spots. Small streams of water are common in almost every valley. There are many types of soil, but in general the clay-rich earth holds plenty of moisture.

Charles Maclaren suggested in his Encyclopedia Britannica article on America that a lack of woodland is the result of a lack of rainfall (Maclaren 1842). However, in this province, abundant, heavy rains fall during the winter and the summers are not excessively dry. Azara also observed that the annual rainfall in these regions is likely greater than that in Spain. Further, I myself observed later in the journey that almost the entirety of Australia is covered by tall trees despite having a much drier climate. Logically, there must be another cause.

Looking only at South America, we are tempted to believe that trees only flourish in very humid climates with plenty of rainfall. After all, the boundaries of the forests match the paths of the winds that carry rain from the ocean.

In the south of the continent, where the moist winds blow east from the Pacific Ocean onto the southwest coast, all the islands are densely covered by impenetrable forests, from southern Chile (latitude 38°) south to Tierra del Fuego. But the air loses its moisture in passing over the towering Andes. Thus, on the southeastern side, the sky is blue, the climate is fine, and the dry plains of Patagonia support little vegetation. When we look to the north of the continent, where the constant trade winds blow onto the east coast,

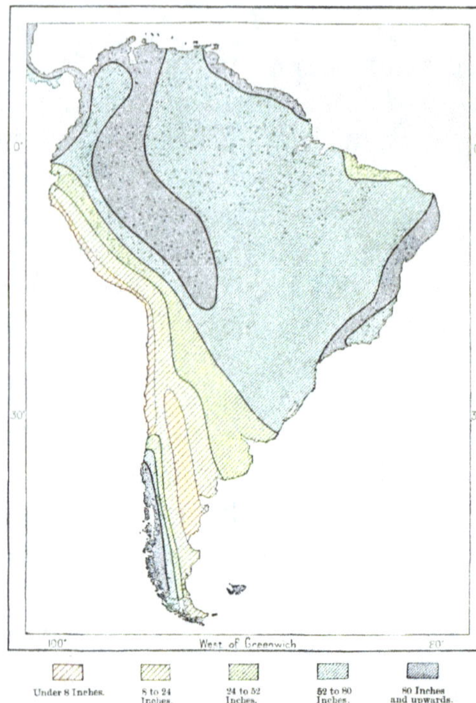

Rainfall patterns in South America. Elisée Reclus, 1894.

we find magnificent forests. Meanwhile, the western coast is a desert from 4° to 32° south latitude. Further north on this same western coast (above 4° south latitude), the trade winds are less constant and heavy torrents of rain fall on the Pacific shores. Near Cabo Blanco, in the extreme north of Peru, the land transforms from utter desert to the luxuriant forest for which Ecuador and Panama are justifiably famous. Simply put, the forests and deserts switch positions in the southern and northern parts of the continent, relative to the Andes. Thus, it appears that the presence of forest or desert depends on the direction of the wind and the rain.

In the middle of the continent there is an intermediate zone, which includes central Chile and the provinces of La Plata. Here, rain-bearing winds do not have to cross high mountains, and the climate is neither desert nor forested.

Yet, every rule has exceptions. Consider the Falkland Islands. They are at the same latitude as Tierra del Fuego, located just 200–300 miles away, and share a similar climate, geological makeup, and peaty soil. Yet, the Falklands have only small plants that barely qualify as bushes, whereas in Tierra del Fuego it is impossible to find an acre of land not covered in dense forest.

This difference is puzzling. Strong winds and ocean currents could easily carry seeds from Tierra del Fuego to the Falklands. After all, canoes and tree trunks from Tierra del Fuego often wash up on the Falklands' shores. Many other kinds of plants are already found in both places. However, attempts to transplant trees from Tierra del Fuego to the Falklands consistently fail.

Animals Collected

Pampas deer (*Ozotoceros bezoarticus*) are the only large native mammal still common in the La Plata region. Rowland Ward, 1898.

During the ten weeks that we stay in Maldonado, I collect several mammals, 80 bird species, and many reptiles, including nine snake species.

Deer

The only large native mammal still commonly found here is the pampas deer (*Ozotoceros bezoarticus*). This deer is exceedingly abundant and often found in small herds throughout the regions bordering the Plata River and northern Patagonia. When I crawl low to the ground and slowly approach a herd, the deer typically draw closer out of curiosity to observe me. Using this method, I once kill three deer from the same herd while remaining in a single spot. Despite their tame and inquisitive nature, they become highly wary when approached on horseback. In this region, where no one travels on foot, the deer recognize humans as enemies only when mounted and armed with *bolas*.

At Bahía Blanca, a recently established settlement in northern Patagonia, I am surprised to see that the deer seem indifferent to the sound of a gunshot. On one occasion, I fire ten times at a deer from within 80 yards, and it reacts more to the dirt kicked up by the bullets than to the loud crack of my rifle. To my embarrassment as a sportsman, though I am skilled at shooting birds in flight, I eventually have to stand up and shout to scare it away after my gunpowder is exhausted.

The most curious fact about this animal is the overpoweringly strong and offensive smell of the male deer, or buck. It is utterly indescribable. While skinning a specimen, I am repeatedly overcome with nausea from the stench. This specimen is now mounted at the Museum of Zoology at the University of Cambridge. I wrap the skin in a silk pocket-handkerchief to carry it home. Even after using and washing the handkerchief many times, the smell lingers. For a full year and seven months, whenever I unfold the handkerchief, I can still faintly detect the odor. This is a remarkable example of the persistence of a substance that must be highly volatile in nature, which easily evaporates at normal temperatures.

I often perceive the smell of the male deer from as far as half a mile away when passing a herd. The smell of the buck is particularly intense when its horns are fully developed and free from the velvety skin that covers them at other times. At this stage, the meat is entirely inedible. However, the *gauchos* claim that burying the meat in fresh earth for some time removes the taint. Interestingly, I have read that islanders in northern Scotland use a similar method to make the rank carcasses of fish-eating birds palatable.

Rodents

The Rodentia order, the group that includes gnawing animals like rats and mice, is remarkably diverse in this region. During my time in South America, I collect 27 species of mice, eight of which are found here, nearly a third of the total number of species I find!

Capybara

The largest rodent in the world, the capybara, or water-hog (*Hydrochoerus hydrochaeris*), is common in this region. I shoot a capybara near Montevideo that weighs 98 pounds. Its length is three feet two inches measured from snout to tail, and its girth is three feet eight inches around the middle.

Capybaras sometimes visit the islands at the mouth of the Plata River, where the water is quite salty. However, they are far more abundant along the edges of freshwater lakes and rivers. Near Maldonado, they usually live in groups of three or four. During the day, they rest among aquatic plants or graze openly on grassy plains.

From a distance, their manner of walking and coloring make them look like pigs. But when they sit upright on their haunches and watch their surroundings with one eye, they resemble their smaller relatives, cavies and rabbits. Their deep jaws make them look ludicrous from both the side and front views.

These animals are easy to kill, but their skins are of little value, and their meat is not particularly tasty. They are extremely

Capybara (*Hydrochoerus hydrochaeris*), a huge aquatic rodent that lives in groups. Gustav Mützel, 1800s.

abundant on the islands of the Río Paraná, and serve as the main prey for the jaguar.

The capybaras near Maldonado are surprisingly tame. By moving cautiously, I once approach within three yards of four adults. This tameness is likely because jaguars, their primary predator, have been absent in the area for years, and the *gauchos* do not think it is worthwhile to hunt them. As I approach nearer and nearer, the capybaras repeatedly make their peculiar sound—a low grunt produced by a sudden burst of air. It reminds me of the sound of a large dog waking up from a nap and giving a hoarse bark with more air than sound. I watch them (and they watch me) for several minutes before they impetuously gallop into the water at full speed, barking as they jump. After diving under the water and swimming a short distance away, they resurface with only the tops of their heads poking out of the water. I hear that the babies sit on the back of their mother as she swims.

When I dissect a capybara, I find that its stomach and intestines contain a thin yellowish fluid, with no visible plant fibers. A closer look at the animal's neck reveals that the esophagus is too narrow for anything larger than the width of a crow quill to pass through. Their broad teeth and strong jaws must be well suited to thoroughly grind aquatic plants into pulp before swallowing.

Tuco-tuco

Tuco-tucos (*Ctenomys brasiliensis*) are a strange little animal that combine the traits of a rodent with the underground lifestyle of a mole. These creatures are

Tuco-tuco. Anonymous, 1800s.

extremely common in some parts of the country, but they are difficult to capture because they never leave their burrows. At the entrance of their tunnels, they create mounds of dirt, similar to molehills but smaller. Large areas are so completely dug up by these animals that horses walking over the fields sink up to their ankles.

Tuco-tucos appear to be gregarious since I usually see them in groups. The man who catches specimens for me captured six together at one time, which he says is quite common. These animals are nocturnal, being most active at night. Their primary diet consists of plant roots, which is why they dig their extensive, shallow tunnels.

Everyone knows the tuco-tuco by its peculiar call, which sounds like the name. The noise is a short, nasal grunt that is quickly repeated about four times. The first time I hear it, I am quite startled. I cannot tell where the sound comes from or guess that kind of animal makes it. In areas where these animals are abundant, you can hear them calling all day from under the ground, sometimes even directly beneath your feet!

I keep several alive in a room to observe them. Some of them become tame after only a day and stop trying to bite or run away, though a few remain wild and wary. They move slowly and clumsily, probably because their hind legs move outward rather than directly backward. I notice that they are incapable of jumping even the smallest height because their thigh bone socket lacks a certain ligament. This makes them appear quite stupid when they try to escape. When frightened or angry, they just say "tuco-tuco!"

Interestingly, my collecting assistant asserts that many tuco-tucos are blind. To test this, I put my finger half an inch from the face of a tuco-tuco and note that the animal does not react. However, it navigates the room nearly as well as the others. The Scottish anatomist John Reid kindly examined a blind specimen I preserved in alcohol. He tells me that the tuco-tuco's blindness is probably caused by an inflamed nictitating membrane (a thin, clear tissue that protects the eye in many animals, also known as the third eyelid). Considering their entirely subterranean lifestyle, blindness may not be a significant disadvantage for tuco-tucos.

This raises an intriguing question: why would an animal possess an organ—its eye—that is so often injured? The naturalist Jean-Baptiste Lamarck, who believes in the absurd idea that species evolve by inheriting traits acquired by their parents, would be delighted by the tuco-tuco. He speculates that animals like *Spalax* (blind-mole rats) and *Proteus* (cave salamanders) gradually lost their eyesight over time (Lamarck 1809). Both of these creatures now have rudimentary eyes covered by membranes or skin. In comparison, common moles have very small but functional eyes. Though some anatomists believe that their eyes are not connected to their optic nerves, vision would certainly be useful to them when they leave their burrow. Lamarck might suggest that tuco-tucos are on their way to evolving into a state similar to that of the *Spalax* or *Proteus* as their eyes become increasingly unnecessary in their underground world.

Birds

Cowbird with Cuckoo-like Behavior

The rolling, grassy plains near Maldonado are full of birds. There are several species that resemble English starlings in both structure and behavior. One of these species is the shiny cowbird (*Molothrus bonariensis*), notable for their unusual behavior. I often see groups of these birds perched on cows or horses, or preening themselves on sunny hedges. They occasionally try to sing, though it sounds more like a hiss. This peculiar high-pitched sound is similar to air bubbles escaping rapidly from a thin tube underwater.

According to the naturalist Azara, cowbirds lay their eggs in the nests of other birds, as does the cuckoo. I find evidence for this here. Many country people tell me about a bird who lays eggs in the nests of other birds. My collecting assistant, who is a very accurate observer, eventually finds a sparrow nest (*Zonotrichia capensis*) with one egg that is larger and has a different color and shape than the rest of the eggs.

A closely related species in North America, the brown-headed cowbird (*Molothrus ater*), behaves in much the same way. They are strikingly similar to shiny cowbirds—they even have the same habit of standing on cattle. They are just slightly smaller and their feathers and eggs are a different color. Though common in nature, this concordance between appearance and behavior of different species on opposite sides of a continent always strikes me as interesting.

In his study on the natural history of cuckoos, William Swainson remarks that very few birds can truly be called parasitical. Aside from cuckoos and cowbirds, no others "fasten themselves" to another living creature to such an extent. These birds depend on their host's warmth to hatch their eggs and on their foster parents' care to raise their young. Without the host, the parasitical bird's young would not survive (Swainson 1836).

Although alike in being brood-parasites, their other

Cowbird (*Molothrus bonariensis*). Carl Wilhelm Hahn, 1800s.

behaviors are vastly different. Cowbirds, like English starlings, are highly sociable and live in open plains without concealment. In contrast, cuckoos are shy birds that hide in dense thickets, feeding on fruit and caterpillars. Structurally, the two birds are quite distinct as well.

Scientists propose various theories to explain why cuckoos lay eggs in other birds' nests. These include phrenological ideas about their instincts suggesting that their skull shape might inform us about their character. However, only the French ornithologist Florent Prévost throws real light on this puzzle. He observes that female cuckoos lay up to six eggs in a season, but can lay only one or two eggs at a time. Between each laying, she must pair with a male again. This makes it impossible for a female cuckoo to incubate her eggs herself. She would either have to sit on all of them at once, leaving the first-laid eggs so long they would rot, or sit on just one or two eggs at a time, which would take far too long. Cuckoos spend less time in their migratory breeding grounds than most birds, so they would simply not have enough time to incubate their eggs. It is because the female must pair between each laying that it is necessary for her to leave her eggs in the nests of other birds, this ensures her young can hatch and grow in the care of foster-parents (Prévost 1834).

I am strongly inclined to believe Prévost's explanation because I notice a similar behavior among South American rheas. Female rheas, in a sense, act as parasites to each other. Each lays her eggs in the nests of several other females, while the male rhea takes on the role of incubating all the eggs. This unique system shares a resemblance to the cuckoo's habit of relying on foster parents to rear its young.

Cuckoo (*Cuculus canorus*). William Foster, 1922.

Tyrant-flycatcher

I will mention only two other common birds that stand out for their peculiar behavior. One of them is the great kiskadee (*Pitangus sulphuratus*), a classic example of the large American family of tyrant-flycatchers. Their structure closely resembles shrikes, but their behavior mimics several kinds of birds at once. I often see them hunting in fields, hovering over one spot like a hawk. When I see them at a distance, suspended in the air, I could easily mistake them for a bird of prey. However, their dive is much less forceful and swift than that of a true hawk. Sometimes, I find tyrant-flycatcher near water acting like kingfishers. They perch motionless before darting to catch small fish near the water's edge. The flight of the tyrant-flycatcher is distinctively wavy—it looks like their large heads and bills are too heavy for their bodies. In the evenings, they usually perch on roadside bushes and repeat a high-pitched call. While shrill, it is rather agreeable. The sound is so distinctive that the Spaniards think it resembles the phrase, "*Bien te veo*" ("I see you well"), which is why they give the bird this name.

People like to keep these birds as pets, either in cages or courtyards, with their wings clipped. They quickly become tame and are entertaining to watch, with behavior described as mischievous and clever, similar to magpies.

The behavior of the great kiskadee (*Pitangus sulphuratus*) mimics several kinds of birds at once. Joseph Wolf, 1850.

Mockingbird

Locally known as *calandrias*, chalk-browed mockingbirds (*Mimus saturninus*) stand out for their extraordinary song which surpasses that of any other bird in the region. In fact, they are almost the only bird in South America that perches specifically to sing. Their melody is comparable to the sedge warbler, but *calandrias* sing more powerfully, blending harsh and high-pitched notes with a pleasant, warbling tone. They only sing in the spring. At other times, their cry is harsh and far from melodious.

Near Maldonado, these birds are bold and unafraid. There are always many of them at the country houses, flocking to pick at meat hung on walls or posts. They chase away any smaller birds that dare to join the feast.

When I visit the vast, uninhabited plains of Patagonia, I encounter another species of mockingbird that the French naturalist Alcide d'Orbigny describes as *Mimus patagonicus*. This species lives in valleys covered with spiny bushes. It is wilder and has a different voice than the Maldonado species.

Curiously, when I first see the Patagonian species I immediately recognize it as different from the Maldonado species based on these slight differences in habitat and behavior. However, when I carelessly compare my specimens later, they look so similar that I change my mind. Now, thanks to the expertise of the leading British ornithologist John Gould, I know they are indeed distinct species. His conclusion aligns with my initial observation of their slight differences in behavior, even though he was unaware of this at the time.

Calandrias (*Mimus saturninus*) stand out for their extraordinary song. Alcide d'Orbigny, 1847.

Carrion Hawks

South American carrion-feeding hawks strike me as far more numerous, tame, and disgusting than European birds. Among them are four caracara species, as well as turkey vultures, *gallinazos*, and condors.

Caracaras

Caracaras are classified as eagles based on their physical structure, but we shall soon see how poorly they live up to such a high rank. Based on their behavior, I should say they take the place of crows, magpies, and ravens, which are widely distributed in many parts of the world but entirely absent in South America.

Caracara plancus is the most common and widespread of the four caracara species. The locals call them *caranchos*. This bird thrives in diverse environments, from the grassy savannas of La Plata to the arid plains of Patagonia. It even inhabits the dense, wet forests of western Patagonia and Tierra del Fuego. I observe them lining the desert road between the Negro and Colorado rivers, ready to devour the carcasses of animals that die from thirst and exhaustion.

We frequently find *caranchos* and their smaller relatives, *chimangos* (*Milvago chimango*), in great numbers at *estancias* (what they call ranches here) and slaughterhouses. These birds gather to scavenge dead animal carcasses alongside *gallinazos*. After *gallinazos* begin the feast, *caranchos* and *chimangos* often finish by picking the bones clean. Though they dine together, these scavengers are far from friendly toward one another. I regularly see *chimangos* harass resting *caranchos*, flying back and forth in semicircles and striking at the larger bird, which responds with little more than a bob of its head.

Caranchos are known for being crafty and stealing large numbers of eggs from other birds. They also peck at the sores of horses and mules to remove scabs. The British naval officer who traveled widely in this region, Captain Francis Head, vividly describes the poor beasts standing with ears down and back arched while the bird hovers nearby, eyeing its disgusting morsel.

They are false eagles that rarely hunt live prey. Their necrophagous, or carrion-eating, tendencies are chilling to anyone who has wandered over the desolate plains of Patagonia. More than once, I wake from a nap to see these birds perched on nearby hills, watching me with an evil eye. Several of these hawks shadow our men and dogs when we go hunting, hoping to benefit from our spoils.

These are sluggish, tame, and cowardly birds. *Caranchos* fly slowly and heavily, reminding me of English rooks. They rarely soar, though I twice see one glide gracefully at great heights. On the ground, they run rather than hop, though not as swiftly as some of their relatives. After a meal, I observe their naked craws sticking out, full of meat.

Caranchos have a harsh and peculiar call that sounds much like a Spanish guttural "g" followed by a rough, rolling "rrr." When calling, the bird gradually raises its head and arches its neck until the crown of the head nearly touches its back. Although others doubt it, I myself saw them with beaks wide open and heads inverted.

El carancho, or crested caracara (*Caracara plancus*), is the most common and widespread of the caracara species. John James Audubon, 1800s.

According to Azara, a respected authority, *caranchos* also eat worms, slugs, grasshoppers, frogs, and even shellfish. *Caranchos* are seen killing newborn lambs by tearing their umbilical cords. They also chase *gallinazos* until they vomit up recently eaten carrion. Groups of *caranchos* sometimes hunt large birds such as herons. Though frequently found in large groups, they are not gregarious, as they are often seen in the desert alone or in pairs. This versatility in diet and behavior highlights their ingenuity and adaptability.

The *chimango* (*Milvago chimango*) is the *carancho*'s smaller cousin. David William Mitchell, 1849.

Chimangos are *carancho*'s smaller cousins. This bird is truly omnivorous, eating everything from bread to potatoes. Locals tell me that they harm potato crops by digging up freshly planted roots on Chiloé. Of all the carrion-feeders, *chimangos* are typically the last to leave the remains of a dead animal. We sometimes see them perched within the rib cage of a carcass like birds in a cage.

Falkland Islands Scavenger

Another notable scavenger species is the Forster's caracara (*Phalcoboenus australis*), which is extremely common in the Falkland Islands, off the South American coast. These birds share many behaviors with *caranchos*. They live on dead animals and marine debris. On the isolated Diego Ramírez Islands, they must depend entirely on what the sea throws up on the beach.

Extraordinarily brave birds, they frequently visit human settlements in search of decomposing food and offal. When a hunting party kills an animal, these scavengers gather quickly, patiently waiting for their turn at the carcass. After feeding, their extended craws give them a grotesque appearance. I once see a wounded cormorant on the shore rapidly attacked and killed by several of these birds. Much like *caranchos*, a group of these birds will wait near rabbit holes to catch exiting animals.

Officers of the ship that sailed alongside the *Beagle* on her first expedition, the H.M.S. *Adventure*, report the extreme boldness of the Forster's caracara during winter. The birds once attempted to seize wounded geese immediately after being shot by hunters. The officers were amazed to see one of these birds pounce on a dog sleeping close to his master. The birds went so far as to board the ship when anchored in the harbor, so the sailors had to keep a lookout to stop them from tearing the leather rigging and stealing meat from the stern of the ship.

These birds are also mischievous and inquisitive. They pick up anything left unattended on the ground. They once fly away with a large shiny black hat, a set of heavy balls used in the *bolas*, and even a small compass encased in red leather (a severe loss for my shipmate, officer Alexander Usborne). Their behavior is both quarrelsome and passionate—they are even seen tearing up grass out of apparent rage. Though they are not gregarious, they gather at carcasses. At times, they run quickly on the ground, resembling pheasants. Rather than soaring, their flight is heavy and clumsy. They are noisy and their harsh cries are similar to English rooks, which is what the sealers call them. Curiously, they throw their heads back dramatically when they cry out, much like *caranchos.*

These birds nest in the rocky cliffs along the coast, choosing smaller islets over the main Falkland Islands. This seems like an odd precaution for such a bold species. Sealers claim their meat is white and palatable, but you would need great courage to try it.

A young Forster's caracara (*Phalcoboenus australis*) from the Falkland Islands. Georges Leclerc de Buffon, 1838.

Turkey vultures (*Cathartes aura*) live in damp places throughout South America into North America. John James Audubon, 1838.

Turkey Vulture & Gallinazo

Turkey vultures (*Cathartes aura*) live in damp parts of the countryside from Cape Horn on the southern tip of South America up to North America. Unlike *caranchos* and *chimangos*, they also live in the Falkland Islands. We instantly recognize this solitary bird, even at a distance, by its most elegant, soaring flight high in the air. As most people know, it feeds on carrion, feasting on whatever dead animals it finds. On the thickly wooded little islands and broken lands of the western Patagonian coast, it survives on seal carcasses and debris washed ashore. I see vultures wherever large groups of seals gather on the rocks.

Gallinazos, or black vultures (*Coragyps atratus*) have a different range—they only live north of latitude 41°S. According to Azara, these vultures were originally absent from Montevideo, but migrated there following human settlement into the south of the continent. They may have expanded even further south since Azara's time, as they now populate the valley of the Colorado, 300 miles south of Montevideo. They favor humid climates or areas near fresh water so they are abundant in Brazil and the La Plata region, but they only live near streams on the arid plains of northern

Patagonia. I frequently see them everywhere in the Pampas, all the way to the foot of the Andes, but I never see, or even hear of, one in Chile. In Peru, they are common scavengers.

Gallinazos are truly gregarious, exhibiting a preference for social interaction, not only gathering around prey. On fine days, flocks of them perform graceful aerial displays, wheeling high in the sky with outspread wings. They appear to do this for the pure pleasure of taking exercise, though it is possibly related to mating.

Condor

The magnificent Andean condor (*Vultur gryphus*) is another carrion-feeder, but we will have a full account of this bird when we visit a country more suitable for it than the plains of La Plata.

Gallinazos, or black vultures (*Coragyps atratus*) live further north and prefer a humid climate. John James Audubon, 1838.

Effects of Lightning

Tubes Formed by Lightning

I am utterly fascinated by my discovery of fulgurites, tubes formed when lightning strikes loose sand and transforms it into glass. I find these tubes in the sand dunes separating the Laguna del Potrero from the shores of the Plata River, near Maldonado.

The ever-shifting sands, unprotected by vegetation, exposed the tubes. Some fragments scattered nearby suggest they were once buried more deeply. I find four sets of tubes that entered the sand almost vertically. Curious to know how deep they go, I dig in the sand with my hands until I trace one to a depth of two feet. Then I search for nearby fragments that fit together with the tube I unearthed. When combined, the entire tube plus fragments measures over five feet long. The width of the tube and pieces is even along its length. Assuming that the end must taper, we can suppose that it was originally much longer and deeper. The journal of the Geological Society of London describes tubes such as these that were found near Drigg, on the Irish coast. Though the tube I measure seems long, it is small compared to one of the Drigg tubes, which extended at least thirty feet into the ground.

The inside surface of the tubes is glossy and smooth. When I examine them under a microscope, I see numerous tiny bubbles of air or steam trapped in the glassy walls, resembling the texture of material melted by a blowpipe flame. The tube walls vary from about one-tenth to one-thirtieth of an inch thick. Grains of sand stuck to the outside of the tube are slightly rounded and glazed, but

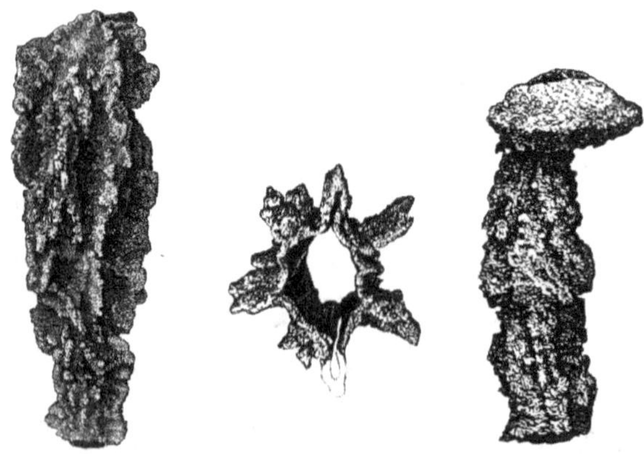

Glassy tubes made by lightning strikes have lengthwise furrows from being compacted by the surrounding sand while still fluid. Anonymous, 1886.

not crystallized. The sand grains are completely, or mostly, siliceous (quartz-based), though some are black with a shiny, metallic luster.

Similar to what I read in the Geological Society journal, I note deep, lengthwise furrows in the tubes. The furrows are apparently caused by the surrounding sand compressing, or squeezing, the tubes while they are still hot and semi-liquid. Thus, the tubes look like shriveled plant stalks or the rough bark of an elm or cork tree. Most of the tubes measure two inches around, though a few uncompressed fragments are four inches in circumference. The larger fragments suggest that the "bore" of the lightning, if such a term can be used, measured about 1¼ inches in diameter.

Most of the tubes entered the sand vertically. However, one is different from the others. It deviates from a right angle, bending as much as 33°. This one tube also branches in two places—one branch points downward while the other bends upward at an acute angle of 26°. This upward branch is particularly astonishing, as it suggests the electric current reversed its direction!

The most remarkable thing is that I find several tubes together in a small space. All the tubes are located in a level area of shifting sand measuring about 20 by 60 yards. This area is about half a mile from a row of hills that are 500–600 feet high. Altogether, I find fragments of at least four tubes. Similarly, three tubes were found within 15 yards at Drigg. Johann Friedrich Ribbentrop documented a similar number in Germany. It seems improbable that lightning repeatedly struck the ground in the same place. This clustering therefore suggests that lightning often divides into separate branches before entering the ground.

Two French scientists—physicist Jean Hachette and mineralogist François Beudant—succeeded in making tubes similar to these fulgurites by passing strong electrical shocks through finely-powdered glass. By adding salt, they were able to produce tubes slightly less than one inch long and 2/100th of an inch wide. They failed entirely to make tubes in either feldspar or quartz (Hachette and Beudant 1828).

Consider that the strongest battery in Paris can only make such small tubes in an easily melted material such as glass. Are we not even more astonished by the force of a lightning strike, which can make a tube more than 30 feet long and 1½ inches wide in a material as resistant as quartz?

Struck by Lightning

During our several visits to the Río de la Plata region, we hear of a ship, two churches, and a house being struck by lightning. I examine one church and the house shortly after these events. Alexander Hood is the owner of the house that was struck and the consul-general at Montevideo. The lightning strikes affected the house in curious ways. In Hood's house, I note that the wallpaper near the bell wires is scorched, with black marks extending almost a foot on either side. The metal bell wires melted entirely. Though the room is around fifteen feet high, the molten droplets of metal that fell drilled a row of tiny holes in the chairs and furniture below. Part of one wall is completely shattered, as if exploded by gunpowder, and fragments were blown across the room with enough energy to dent the opposite wall. The metal gilding on a mirror frame was apparently evaporated by the intense heat. The volatilized particles then fell onto a small bottle to which the metallic particles adhered firmly, as if they had been painted on.

The La Plata region seems especially prone to lightning strikes. In 1793, one of the most destructive thunderstorms on record hit Buenos Aires. In one night, lightning struck thirty-seven locations, killing nineteen people. From accounts in various travel books, I suspect that thunderstorms are more common near the mouths of large rivers. Could it be that the mixing of large bodies of fresh and salt water disrupts the electrical equilibrium in the atmosphere?

Ship struck twice by lightning in the La Plata region. William Elliott, 1786.

Sailing South to the Río Negro

As the *Beagle* weighs anchor to sail south towards the Río Negro in Argentina, I ponder unanswered questions about lighting, and wonder what lies ahead of us. Will we experience electrical storms and other dangers as we sail along the lonely South American coast? All I know is that the voyage ahead promises great adventure and my anticipation of new discoveries increases with every mile we travel.

The ship weighs anchor and sails south to new adventures. Anonymous, 1864.

Continue the Voyage

Book 1: Our journey aboard the *Beagle* has only just begun. In this first book, we followed him across the Atlantic to the tropical forests of Brazil and the sweeping plains of Uruguay. But our greatest adventures are yet to come.

Book 2: We travel to Argentina, where we join young Charles as he explores vast, empty plains, hunts giant fossil bones, and learns how to use *bolas* from the legendary *gauchos*. He narrowly escapes from the political turmoil in Buenos Aires and then sails south toward the wild landscapes of Patagonia.

Book 3: Young Charles revisits the La Plata region, collecting some of the most important fossils of his journey. Sailing south into Patagonia, he becomes one of the first Europeans to explore the Santa Cruz River. Stopping in the windswept Falkland Islands, he sees mysterious streams of stones and brave penguins. In Tierra del Fuego, we finally learn about the natives Fuegians who have traveled aboard the *Beagle* with him from England. As the ship navigates the Strait of Magellan, he watches glaciers crash into the sea and marvels at how icebergs move boulders.

Book 4: The *Beagle* takes us to the western side of South America, where Charles witnesses the destructive power of a massive earthquake in Chile. We follow him over the towering Andes just before the winter snows arrive. Then we ride across the blistering Atacama Desert in Peru and visit Lima, which suffers from political instability and disease. Along the way, we continue to learn about the evolution of land, animals, and human culture.

Book 5: We reach the most famous stop on our voyage—the Galápagos Islands. Here, Charles collects the legendary finches which later illustrate his theory of evolution by natural selection. From there, we continue across the Pacific to Tahiti, New Zealand, and Australia, encountering dramatic landscapes and traditional cultures. On a brief visit to the Keeling Islands, Charles becomes fascinated by the formation of coral atolls. After exploring Mauritius and South Africa, we sail again across the Atlantic to complete the circumnavigation of the globe before finally returning to England.

Each book is packed with stunning illustrations that bring Darwin's adventures to life. Where will *you* go next?

Name Changes

Currency Conversion Note
I convert money to modern amounts based on purchasing power, where £1 in the 1830s is roughly $100 USD in 2025.

Chapter 1
Name in original text → Modern name
- Captain Fitz Roy → Captain FitzRoy
- Cherty rock → Chert rock
- Diodon antennatus → *Chilomycterus antennatus*
- Felspathic rock → Feldspathic rock
- Fernando Noronha → Fernando de Noronha
- Infusoria with siliceous shields → Diatoms
- Marchantiae → *Marchantia* (Liverworts)
- Nulliporae → Rhodoliths
- Peak of Teneriffe → Mt. Teide
- Porto Praya → Porto Praia
- St. Domingo → São Domingos
- St. Jago → Santiago
- St. Paul's Rock → Saint Peter and Saint Paul Archipelago (St. Paul)
- Teneriffe → Tenerife

Chapter 2
Name in original text → Modern name
- Ampullariae → Pomacea
- Arachnidae → Arachnida
- Brachelytra → Staphylinidae
- Cabbage palm → Açaí palm (*Euterpe oleracea*)
- Engenhodo → Engenho do Mato
- *Epeira clavipes* → *Trichonephila clavipes*
- *Epeira conica* → *Cyclosa conica*
- *Epeira* golden orb-weaving spider → *Leucauge argyrobapta*
- *Epeira tuberculata* → *Glyptogona sextuberculata*
- *Februa hoffmannseggia* → *Historis acheronta*
- Gavia → Pedra da Gávea
- *Hymenophallus* → *Phallus*
- Ithacaia → Itacuruçá
- *Lampyris occidentalis* → *Photuris versicolor*
- Large *Epeira*, related to *E. tuberculata* and *E. conica* → *Argiope argentata*
- Limnaea → Lymnaea
- Mandetiba → Mangaratiba
- *Papilio feronia* → *Hamadryas feronia*
- *Pyrophorus luminosus*, Illig. → *Ignelater luminosus*
- *Pyrosma* → *Pyrosoma*
- *Rhyncophora* → *Rhynchophorus*
- Socego → Sossêgo

- *Strongylus* → *Darwinilus sedarisi*
- Van Dieman's Land → Tasmania
- Yagouaroundi → Jaguarundi (*Puma yagouaroundi*)

Chapter 3
Name in original text → Modern name
- *Asphalax* → Blind mole rat (*Spalax*)
- Cape Blanco → Cabo Blanco
- Capybara (*Hydrochaerus capybara*) → Capybara (*Hydrochoerus hydrochaeris*)
- Deer (*Cervus campestris*) → Pampas deer (*Ozotoceros bezoarticus*)
- Ramirez Rocks → Diego Ramírez Islands
- *Gallinazo* (*Cathartes atratus*) → Gallinazo (*Coragyps atratus*)
- *Mimus orpheus* → *Mimus saturninus*
- Mocking-bird (*O. Patagonica*) d'Orbigny → Patagonian mockingbird (*Mimus patagonicus*)
- *Molothrus niger* → Shiny cowbird (*Molothrus bonariensis*)
- *Molothrus pecoris* → Brown-headed cowbird (*Molothrus ater*)
- *Nothura majo* → *Nothura maculosa*
- *Polyborus Brasiliensis* →Crested caracara (*Caracara plancus*)
- *Saurophagus sulphuratus* → Great kiskadee (*Pitangus sulphuratus*)
- Sparrow (*Zonotrichia matutina*) → Rufous-collared sparrow (*Zonotrichia capensis*)
- *Struthio rhea* → Common rhea (*Rhea americana*)
- Tucutuco (*Ctenomys Brasiliensis*) → Tuco-tuco (*Ctenomys brasiliensis*)
- Turkey-buzzard (*Vultur aura*) → Turkey vulture (*Cathartes aura*)
- Varying Hare → Snowshoe hare (*Lepus americanus*)
- *Verbena melindres* → *Verbena peruviana*

A large and active crab on St. Paul's rocks (*Grapsus pictus*) is so bold that it even drags young birds out of their nests to eat them. Acarie Boren, 1800s.

Image Credits

Anonymous. 1899. An orchid (*Dendrobium farmerii* var. *album*): flowering stem. In Wellcome Collection. CC BY 4.0. Edits: background removed, digitally enhanced.

Anonymous. 1899. *Laelia grandis tenebrosa*. In Wellcome Collection. CC BY 4.0. Edits: cropped, background removed, digitally enhanced.

Anonymous. 1905. An orchid (*Laelia* "Mrs Gratrix"): flowering stem. In Wellcome Collection. CC BY 4.0. Edits: cropped, background removed, digitally enhanced.

Anonymous. 1800s. *Cattleya gigas Sauderiana*. In Wellcome Collection. CC BY-SA 4.0. Edits: cropped, background removed, digitally enhanced.

Anonymous. 1800s. *Cattleya Boothiana*. In Wellcome Collection. CC BY-SA 4.0. Edits: cropped, background removed, digitally enhanced.

Escure, Nathalie. 2003. A representative individual from the soldier caste of the new world army ant species (*Eciton burchellii*) with characteristically shaped mandibles. In *Army Ants Trapped by Their Evolutionary History. oS Biol.* by F. Delsuc. CC BY 2.5. Edits: cropped, background removed, digitally enhanced, colorized.

Heade, Martin Johnson. 1800s. Two hummingbirds and an orchid, Brazil. CC BY 2.0. Edits: cropped, digitally enhanced.

Keulemans, John Gerrard. 1868. Grey-headed Kingfisher (*Halcyon leucocephala*). In *A Monograph of the Alcedinidae, or Family of Kingfishers* by Richard Bowdler Sharpe. Plate 64. CC BY 2.0. Edits: cropped, background removed, digitally enhanced.

Martinet, Francois Nicolas. 1793. The caural snipe. In Wellcome Collection: *The Natural History of Birds* by Count de Buffon. Plate 206. CC BY-SA 4.0. Edits: cropped, background removed, digitally enhanced.

Mignot, Louis Rémy. 1863. Lagoon of the Guayaquil River. CC BY-SA 4.0. Edits: cropped, digitally enhanced.

Rugendas, Johann Moritz. 1832. Habitation de negres. In *Voyage Pittoresque dans le Brésil* by Johann Moritz Rugendas. Plate 5. CC BY 2.0. Edits: cropped, background removed, digitally enhanced, colorized.

Weber, Max. 1890. Planarian. In *Zoologische Ergebnisse einer Reise in Niederländisch Ost-Indien* by Max Weber. Plate 12. CC BY-SA 3.0. Edits: cropped, background removed, digitally enhanced, colorized.

For full image credits with links visit www.rainforestkids.org.

Hydrophilus water beetle. Van der Willigen, 1895.

References Cited

Azara, Félix de. 1809. *Voyages Dans l'Amérique Méridionale.* Vol. 1. Paris.

Darwin, Charles. 1844. "Brief Description of Several Terrestrial Planariae, and of Some Remarkable Marine Species, with an Account of Their Habits." *The Annals and Magazine of Natural History; Zoology, Botany, and Geology* (London) 14: 241–51.

Doubleday, Edward. 1845. "On a Peculiar Structure in the Wings of Feronia Producing Sound." *Transactions of the Entomological Society of London* 4: 123–25.

Dumont d'Urville, Jules-Sébastien-César. 1830. *Voyage de La Corvette l'Astrolabe: Exécuté Par Ordre Du Roi, Pendant Les Années 1826-1827-1828-1829.* J. Tastu.

Duperrey, Louis-Isidore, Arthus Bertrand, Bory de Saint-Vincent, et al. 1826. *Voyage Autour Du Monde: Exécuté Par Ordre Du Roi, Sur La Corvette de Sa Majesté, La Coquille, Pendant Les Années 1822, 1823, 1824, et 1825.* Vol. 1. Arthus Bertrand.

Flinders, Matthew. 1814. *A Voyage to Terra Australis: Undertaken for the Purpose of Completing the Discovery of That Vast Country, and Prosecuted in the Years 1801, 1802 and 1803, in His Majesty's Ship the Investigator, and Subsequently in the Armed Vessel Porpoise and Cumberland Schooner: With an Account of the Shipwreck of the Porpoise, Arrival of the Cumberland at Mauritius, and Imprisonment of the Commander during Six Years and a Half in That Island.* Vol. 2. G. and W. Nicol.

Gay, Claude. 1833. "Aperçu Sur Les Recherches d'histoire Naturelle Faites Dans l'Amérique Du Sud, et Principalement Dans Le Chili, Pendant Les Années 1830 et 1831." *Annales Des Sciences Naturelles* (Paris) 28: 1–490.

Hachette, J. N. P., and F. S. Beudant. 1828. "Expériences Sur La Formation de Tubes Fulminaires." *Annales de Chimie et de Physique* 37: 319–21.

Hearne, Samuel. 1795. *A Journey from Prince of Wales's Fort in Hudson's Bay to the Northern Ocean in the Years 1769, 1770, 1771 & 1772.* A. Strahan and T. Cadell.

Horner, Leonard, and David Brewster. 1836. "On an Artificial Substance Resembling Shell: With an Account of an Examination of the Same." *Philosophical Transactions of the Royal Society of London* 126: 49–56.

Humboldt, Alexander von, and Aimé Bonpland. 1821. *Personal Narrative of Travels to the Equinoctial Regions of the New Continent, during the Years 1799–1804.* Translated by Helen Maria Williams. Vol. 5. Longman, Hurst, Rees, Orme, and Brown.

Hutton, Thomas. 1832. "Notes in Natural History." *Journal of the Asiatic Society of Bengal* 1: 555–59.

King, Philip Parker, Robert Brown, Allan Cunningham, et al. 1827. *Narrative of a Survey of the Intertropical and Western Coasts of Australia Performed between the Years 1818 and 1822.* John Murray.

Kirby, William, and William Spence. 1817. *An Introduction to Entomology: Or, Elements of the Natural History of Insects*. Vol. 2. Longman, Hurst, Rees, Orme, and Brown.

Labillardière, Jacques Julien Houton de. 1800. *Voyage in Search of La Pérouse: Performed by Order of the Constituent Assembly, during the Years 1791, 1792, 1793, and 1794*. Vol. 2. John Stockdale.

Lamarck, Jean-Baptiste. 1809. *Philosophie Zoologique, Ou Exposition Des Considérations Relatives à l'histoire Naturelle Des Animaux*. Vol. 1. Dentu.

Langsdorff, Georg Heinrich von. 1813. *Voyages and Travels in Various Parts of the World during the Years 1803, 1804, 1805, 1806, and 1807*. Vol. 1. Henry Colburn.

Maclaren, Charles. 1842. "America." In *Encyclopaedia Britannica*, 7th ed., vol. 2. Adam & Charles Black.

Montagne, Camille. 1844a. "Mémoire Sur Plusieurs Nouvelles Espèces de Cryptogames." *Annales Des Sciences Naturelles. Botanique* (Paris) 2: 354–69.

Montagne, Camille. 1844b. "Sur Quelques Espèces Nouvelles de Cryptogames." *Comptes Rendus Hebdomadaires Des Séances de l'Académie Des Sciences* (Paris) 18: 772–74.

"On the Vitreous Tubes Found near to Drigg, in Cumberland." 1814. *Transactions of the Geological Society of London* 2: 528–32.

Owen, Richard. 1852. "Cephalopoda." In *The Cyclopaedia of Anatomy and Physiology*, edited by Robert Bentley Todd, vol. 1. Longman, Brown, Green, Longmans, & Roberts.

Péron, François, Louis Claude Desaulses de Freycinet, Charles Alexandre Lesueur, Nicolas-Martin Petit, and Nicolas Baudin. 1807. *Voyage de Découvertes Aux Terres Australes Exécuté Par Ordre de Sa Majesté l'Empereur et Roi Sur Les Corvettes Le Géographe, Le Naturaliste et La Goëlette Le Casuarina Pendant Les Années 1800–1804*. Vol. 2. De l'Imprimerie impériale.

Prévost, Florent. 1834. "Communication Read before the Académie Des Sciences (Paris) on Cuckoo Reproduction." *L'Institut: Journal Universel Des Sciences et Des Sociétés Savantes*, 418.

Priestley, Joseph, John Boddington, Edward Nickson, et al. 1778. "Sundry Papers Relative to an Accident from Lightning at Purfleet, May 15, 1777." *Philosophical Transactions of the Royal Society of London* 68: 232–317.

Swainson, William. 1836. "On the Natural History and Relations of the Family of Cuculidae or Cuckoos, with a View to Determine the Series of Their Variation." *The Magazine of Zoology and Botany* 1: 213–25.

Ulloa, Antonio de, Jorge Juan, and John Adams. 1772. *A Voyage to South America: Describing at Large, the Spanish Cities, Towns, Provinces on That Extensive Continent*. 3rd ed. Lockyer Davis.

White, Adam. 1841. "Descriptions of New or Little Known Arachnida." *The Annals and Magazine of Natural History* 7: 471–77.

About the Author

Dr. Faith Inman has spent her life traveling the world, learning and teaching about nature. She trained as a botanist at North Carolina State University researching forest restoration in Puerto Rico and earned her doctorate at the University of California, Los Angeles studying Hawaiian forest regeneration dynamics. After many years doing research and teaching at the University of Hawai'i, she moved to Costa Rica to live as simply as possible surrounded by trees. There she sees many of the same species that Charles Darwin wrote about. Now she is inspired to make scientific ideas more accessible to a broader audience.